BORDERLINE PERSONALITY DISORDER MADE SIMPLE

HOW TO CONTROL EMOTIONS WITHOUT DESTROYING YOUR MINDFULNESS RELATIONSHIPS USING DIALECTICAL, COGNITIVE BEHAVIORAL THERAPY, COMMUNICATION SKILLS TRAINING.

PUBLISHED BY

JULIAN BRAIN

Table of Contents

Introduction.. 1

Chapter 1 Understanding the Borderline Personality Disorder......5

Chapter 2 Diagnosis of the Disorder 20

Chapter 3 Effective Treatments and Therapies for Borderline Personality Disorder...32

Chapter 4 Borderline Personality Disorder Myths Demystified...40

Chapter 5 Diagnosis and Preparation for Your Doctor's Appointment...46

Chapter 6 Inner Therapy 54

Chapter 7 Treatment and Medication 59

Chapter 8 Psychodynamic theory...80

Chapter 9 Find Support for Yourself...92

Chapter 10 The Different Types Of Narcissism...........................116

Conclusion 129

Introduction

What happens when a person has Borderline Personality Disorder? Are there complications that might arise from this condition? If there are, what are they? Everyone deserves to know the risks of Borderline Personality Disorder so that it can be addressed as soon as possible. This condition poses serious problems not only physically and mentally, but also emotionally. If you let it go untreated, you might encounter the worse, and might not be able to recover from it anymore. Thus, it is important that you be informed about the problems that often go along with Borderline Personality Disorder.

Borderline Personality Disorder co-exists with other physical, mental, and emotional problems. Some of them are as follow:

Depression. Depression is a condition characterized by extreme sadness and anxiety. It affects many aspects of one's life. Depression could either last for a short period of time or for a long one. It is associated with persistent sad and anxious feelings, feelings of hopelessness, restlessness, irritability, loss of interest in a lot of activities, difficulty concentrating, fatigue, insomnia, overeating, headaches, and many more. A person with Borderline Personality Disorder experiences depression from time to time, and this may result to suicidal behavior if not addressed as soon as possible.

Eating Disorder. Eating disorder is a common problem encountered when a person is experiencing Borderline Personality Disorder. This is a psychological condition in which a person experiences abnormal eating habits such as excessive or insufficient food intake. This poses detrimental concern both to the mental and physical health of a person. Some of the most common types of eating disorder is bulimia, anorexia, and binge eating disorder. To an extent, this condition can lead to more serious health conditions such as malnourishment or obesity, which in turn may affect the overall health of an individual. Eating disorder can be addressed by seeking help from a medical and psychological expert that would inform you about how to maintain a healthy and consistent eating habit.

Substance Abuse. Substance abuse is more commonly known as drug abuse. This is a condition in which a person uses too much of a substance or a drug to the point that it becomes harmful to one's health, as well as to how an individual deal with other people. People with Borderline Personality Disorder tend to resort to substance abuse whenever they feel that it is the only way to keep themselves from thinking about their problems. They also tend to become dependent to substance whenever they want to get attention. It is normal for them to keep people worried because that is how they want others to treat them. If little or insufficient attention is given, they rely on drugs and alcohol even more, not minding the serious consequences of their actions.

Bipolar Disorder. Manic depressive illness or bipolar disorder is an abnormal condition of the brain. As a result, a person who has bipolar disorder experience unusual mood swings and unnecessary shifts in energy level, interest, and ability to do many things. Bipolar disorder affects many aspects of the life of a person including his relationships with other people, his job or career, and many more. It is characterized by frequent mood swings, extreme irritability, long periods of sadness, loss of interest in particular activities, difficulty concentrating, memory loss, sleeplessness, suicidal behavior, impulsive behavior, restlessness, and changes in one's sleeping and eating habits. This may seem like a hopeless condition, but it can actually be treated through proper medication.

Anxiety Disorder. Although there are cases in which anxiety is necessary and beneficial, there are also circumstances when it is already too much. Excessive anxiety is known as anxiety disorder. There are different kinds of anxiety disorder. Some of them are: generalized anxiety disorder, panic disorder, post-traumatic stress disorder, social phobia, and obsessive-compulsive disorder. These are the most common kinds of anxiety disorder. You can tell whether or not a person is experiencing anxiety disorder when excessive anxiety is still persistent after six months or more. There are different signs and symptoms of anxiety disorder depending on the kind of disorder that a person is suffering from. Despite these characteristics, it is still possible to treat anxiety disorder through therapies and medications.

The risks and complications of Borderline Personality Disorder can even get worse. It can lead to serious health problems such as diseases in the heart, lungs and liver. It can also worsen one's psychological, emotional, and mental condition. Thus, it is important that one is able to identify ways in which these conditions can be addressed properly and effectively.

Chapter 1 Understanding the Borderline Personality Disorder

The borderline personality disorder is recognized as a mental disorder because of its pervasive and inflexible pattern and pathological behavior that is often observed during the early years of a patient but can also persist all throughout his or her life. In this, a discussion of the signs, symptoms and causes of borderline personality disorder will be given.

Signs and Symptoms of Borderline Personality Disorder

The most important symptom of borderline personality disorder is the extreme sensitivity towards rejection. They are also unable to regulate their emotions thus they are impulsive by nature. Below are the signs of symptoms of a patient who is suffering from this condition:

- Emotional instability: People suffering from this condition often tend to have emotions that persist for a long time. This means that people who have this condition find it difficult to stabilize their emotions following an intense emotional experience.

- Out-of-control emotions: They also feel a wide variety of intense emotions. This means that people who have borderline personality disorder may feel overwhelmed with their emotions thus leading them to feel intense grief instead of sadness or intense humiliation than mild embarrassment.

- Tendency to think in black and white: A person with borderline personality disorder has extreme opinions about anything – good or bad. For instance, if a person is supportive to a borderline individual, the person with borderline personality disorder regards him or her as a savior. But if a borderline perceives someone as bad, then he or she will regard that person as extremely evil.

- Intense concern about abandonment: People who suffer from borderline personality disorder hate isolation, rejection and perceived failure. They don't have good coping mechanisms thus when threatened by rejection, they tend to inflict injury upon themselves.

- Unable to tolerate isolation: A borderline individual feels desperate when isolated for a long time. They feel intense panic when they miss a particular family member whom they trust. As a result, the patient results to experiencing dissociation as a defense mechanism during times of isolation.

- Self-damaging behavior: Their inability to react violently over negative things can cause them to do self-damaging things. In fact, people who suffer from borderline personality disorder are prone to having suicidal behavior or self-mutilation. Studies indicate that the suicide rate of people suffering from this disorder is between 3% and 10%.

- Always feeling betrayed by others: People who suffer from this condition feel always that they are out of control with their emotions. They often feel as though their loved ones have betrayed them thus they nurse their hurt which can lead them to think more negative things.

- Impulsivity: Being impulsive is a quality that is common among people who suffer from borderline personality disorder. Because of this, they are prone to alcohol abuse, eating disorders and reckless driving. The behavior of being impulsive provides people with borderline personality disorder a feeling of immediate relief from all of their emotional pains. This means that once they feel guilt, shame or anger, they succumb to any impulsive activity to escape their pain.

- Poor interpersonal relationship: People suffering from borderline personality disorder are very sensitive on the way other treat them. This means that they feel intense joy to people showing them kindness and they also show intense negative reaction to perceived criticisms. This makes it difficult for people with this condition to have good and healthy relationship with others. They tend to be insecure, ambivalent and avoidant to their partners. However, they still desire intimacy; their insecurity makes it difficult for them to truly connect with other people.

- They have manipulative tendencies: People suffering from this condition have manipulative tendencies. They manipulate other people in order to be nurtured or to get positive energy from them.

- Tendency to turn facts around: To get the sympathy of other people, people with borderline personality disorder usually turn facts around to their advantage. This makes them difficult to work with.

- Lack of focus: Their intense emotion makes it difficult for them to have focus and concentration. They also have the tendency to zone out or dissociate once they are overwhelmed with a lot of emotions that require them to react. Their ability to block their mind to avoid feeling intense emotion leads them to be distracted.

A person who is suffering from borderline personality disorder has very distinguishable signs and symptoms thus making them easier to spot than those who are suffering from sociopathy and psychopathy. Moreover, the onset of symptoms occurs more commonly during young adulthood but there are some cases wherein young children were observed to show signs of borderline personality disorder.

Causes of Borderline Personality Disorder

Similar with the case of other personality and mental disorders, the causes of borderline personality disorder are not really fully agreed upon by many experts. There are many psychiatrists and psychologists who link this condition to post-traumatic stress disorder but there are many who link this condition to other factors. This will give a detail discussion about the likely causes why people suffer from borderline personality disorder.

Genetics

Genetics play a vital role in the development of borderline personality disorder. In fact, the heritability of this disorder is shown to be at 65%. Studies indicate that the impulsive aggression among people who are suffering from borderline personality disorder is attributed to serotonin-related genes. On the other hand, researchers are currently studying the 7-repeat polymorphism of the gene dopamine D4 receptor which is linked to the disorganized attachment which is a characteristic common to borderline patients. Moreover, the polymorphisms of the 10/10 dopamine transporter gene have also been linked to the inhibitory controls which patients suffering from borderline personality disorder lacked.

Brain Abnormalities

Neuroimaging studies indicated that reductions of some regions in the brain can affect how the brain regulates emotions. Below are the regions of the brain that can also influence the development of borderline personality disorder.

- Hippocampus: The hippocampus is important in consolidating short term and long term memory. However, studies suggest that a smaller hippocampus can likely cause changes in behavior that can lead to borderline personality disorder.

- Amygdala: The amygdala is smaller in people who have borderline personality disorder. It can also lead to obsessive-compulsive disorder. The amygdala generates all emotions and having a small amygdala can lead to heightened sensitivity and the inability to control emotions of people suffering from personality disorder.

- Prefrontal cortex: The prefrontal cortex is less active for people who are suffering from borderline personality disorder. This is especially true when they recall memories of rejection or abandonment. The inactivity occurs particularly on the anterior cingulated that regulates emotional arousal in response to stress.

- Hypothalamic pituitary adrenal axis: This part of the brain controls the production of cortisol which is the stress hormone. In fact, people who suffer from this condition have hyperactive hypothalamic pituitary adrenal axis thus their brains produce elevated levels of cortisol thus they experience greater stress response than normal people. This also contributes to the irritability of people who suffer from borderline personality disorder.

Biochemical Anomalies

This factor refers to the hormonal imbalance in the body. Many researchers have accounted the development of borderline personality disorder towards the different hormone levels in the body. For instance, high levels of estrogen can cause symptoms of borderline personality disorder to manifest such as mood swings and depression.

Traumatic Childhood Experiences

There is a link between borderline personality disorders to traumatic childhood experiences such as sexual abuse. In fact, many people who suffer from this condition have a history of abuse and neglect from their caregivers when they were young. It has been suggested that chronic abuse and maltreatment can lead to attachment difficulties which is one of the symptoms of borderline personality disorder.

The causes of borderline personality disorder and while genetic play an important role for its development; the environmental factors can also have great influence on its development. The varied causes of borderline personality disorder indicate that this particular condition is as complex as it can be.

Subtypes of Borderline Personality Disorder

Theodore Millon, a famed psychiatrist, proposed four subtypes or categories of borderline personality disorder. This suggests that people who suffer from this condition do not display the same symptoms. Having said this, this makes it challenging to conclude whether a person suffers from borderline personality disorder unless tests are performed. Below is a summary of the different subtypes of this particular personality disorder.

Category	Features
Discouraged	This particular type of borderline personality disorder has avoidant features. They are also plaint, humble and very submissive. They always feel vulnerable and they think that their lives are always in danger. Their avoidant behavior makes them feel hopeless, powerless and depressed at all times.

Petulant	People who are categorized under this subtype have negativistic attitudes towards everything. They are also impatient, defiant, stubborn and resentful. They are quickly disillusioned and are always pessimistic.
Impulsive	This subtype is characterized with histrionic and antisocial behaviors. They are also very capricious, seductive and distractible. People under this subtype are easily agitated, irritable and are high risks of becoming suicidal.
Self-destructive	People who are under this category show depressive as well as masochistic behavior. They are inward turning and always angry. They are also deferential and moody thus they have higher rates of suicide than other subtypes.

Although there are four subtypes identified for borderline personality disorder, it is important to take note that this particular condition is also comorbid with other conditions. In fact, the borderline personality disorder is lifetime comorbid with conditions such as the following below:

- Mood disorders like bipolar disorder and depression

- Anxiety disorders such as social anxiety disorder, panic disorder and post-traumatic stress disorder

- Attention deficit hyperactivity disorder

- Eating disorders such as bulimia and anorexia

- Substance abuse related to drugs and alcoholic substances

A study conducted in 2008 indicated that 75% of people suffering from borderline personality disorder suffer from depression and bipolar disorder. The comorbidity of borderline personality disorder with other personality and mental disorders makes it very difficult to diagnose the condition idling a Coping Skills Toolkit. We all have good days and we all have bad days. Experiencing either can be far more intense if you have BPD. We've talked in about coping skills and the types of skill that can help you to get through more difficult times. A coping skills set will be worth building to help you quickly find ways to deal with bad (or several) days as they arise. Think of this as your Coping Skills Toolkit. This doesn't have to be a physical toolkit, most of the contents will be conceptual anyway, but you can build a list of "items" to go into this kit and carry it around with you. Sometimes when you are overwhelmed with emotion it can be difficult to remember exactly what your coping skills are, or to think clearly about anything. By keeping your list close to hand you can quickly find a way to deal with your emotions. Below is a list of the types of things you can include.

- Mindfulness skills. In an earlier these deserve to be top of the list. They can be practiced just about anywhere and you can simply use breathing to focus your thoughts and concentrate on being in the moment.

- Grounding skills. Very similar to the above these can simply help you to focus on immediate physical and mental stimuli. Use visual or auditory stimulus to take your mind off the immediate negative emotion. Listen to the sounds around you, not just the obvious, but all the sounds that you can hear. Listen to the way in which they rise and fall – so in a busy street you'll hear the roar of traffic, snippets of conversation, birdsong (perhaps) or the sounds of nearby construction work. As long as it's safe, lose yourself in just the sounds around you for a moment.

- Journal keeping. This is a practice that many with BPD find useful for establishing triggers, evaluating emotions and creating lists of pros and cons. Be expressive in your writing, say whatever you want to and everything that you feel. Sometimes simply expressing yourself in this way can get rid of negative thoughts, without risking alienating others! Don't ever worry about details like spelling, grammar or even making sense. Rant on paper as much as you like!

- Positive actions. Think of useful activities to displace your negative emotions. Cleaning the house/oven or sitting and doing some knitting! In fact, anything that is repetitive and requires concentration is an excellent way to manage your emotions and to reduce your intense experience of these.

These are only very basic ideas for you Coping Skills Toolkit. They can be useful for many people but you may also need to find your own ways to cope with the ups and downs of BPD. The important thing to do is list them, keep them with you and build as long a list as you can. Find activities that you can do when you are in the safety of your own home (knitting, for example) and ones that you can do when you are out and about or at work (simple mindfulness, for example). Have a good mix of these so that whatever the situation you can find a simple coping skill that will be suitable for the situation.

Once you've got your list, practice; not all of the skills will come naturally to you and you may need to persevere with some until they do. By practicing you are also reinforcing good skills in your mind and they will be there when you need them. Over time you'll find that your natural reaction to emotional situations is to use one of your new skills, rather than to take the former, self-destructive route. This, as mentioned at the start of the book, is the point where your BPD will begin to be less of a daily issue and you will be well on the way to recovery.

BPD and Self-Esteem

In most cases of BPD you'll find that low self-esteem is part of the scenery! In many instances BPD begins in adolescence and is the result of neglect or abuse. This is quite frequently emotional neglect and the result of being taught that your views or emotions are not valid. People experiencing low self-esteem often feel that they have little to offer to others or the world in general. There are a number of ways in which to build or rebuild your self-esteem and in this we'll look at some basic methods. While these are basic you should consider using all of them regularly. Gradually building a sense of self-worth is a hard process and can take a long time. These exercises and tasks are small enough to complete easily, regularly and without being too challenging or onerous. As you succeed in each (frequently and regularly) you'll find yourself building a sound foundation for feelings of self-worth and also that you are tackle bigger projects or tasks which further build on this.

- Positive Self-Talk. How do you describe yourself, to yourself? "I'm such an idiot"? "I'm a waste of space"? "I'm not worth knowing"? We all feel like this sometimes but these feelings don't build your self-esteem. It's common when things go wrong to use this kind of "self-talk", more so for those with BPD. Positive self-talk is about repositioning these feelings. You forgot an important appointment? "I've messed up, these things happen!" might be a better statement to make to yourself. "Oh well, it's not the end of the world" is another good one - and it's true. So far, nobody alive (or dead) has made a mistake that resulted in that outcome and the chances are, if it happens, it won't be your fault. Be a bit kinder to yourself.

- Take Control. You don't have to take control of big things to make a difference in life. Tidy a drawer, organize a filing system, redecorate a room. Do something that allows you to plan, then execute, a simple task. Do it step by step so achievements come in one after the other. You can consider bigger projects (like bungee jumps or other personal challenges) as your confidence develops – but small steps are where to start.

- Do some charity or voluntary work. This is hugely beneficial, as it's all about giving back to society and feeling useful. This can help you to develop a sense that you have some worth to the world and it also gets you out and about amongst other people. This in itself can be challenging but making new friends and developing broader horizons can be a big boost to your self-esteem.

- Finally, go to your therapy sessions. Everything in this book is aimed towards giving you simple, basic ideas to get you through one day at a time with BPD. However, professional therapy sessions will be where you make your biggest progress and they will, if you attend regularly, not only help you to improve yourself esteem, prove that you can take control of the condition but also help to your final recovery.

Last Words.

The aim of this book is to give you practical, simple and useful techniques to manage BDP on a day-to-day basis. I hope you have found the information and the steps in each useful and helpful. BPD is a common condition but, of all mental or emotional issues, it is one that has the best chances of long term and sustainable recovery. It can take years to recover fully but it's important to set that goal from the start. If you suffer from BDP, or you have recently been diagnosed, it's also important to remember that emotions are not, in themselves, bad. They are important parts of our psychological make-up and essential in our daily lives. Learning to accept them, regulate them and cope with extreme emotions can be hard but it is not an impossible task!

Chapter 2 Diagnosis of the Disorder

One of the hardest things to do with this kind of disorder is to diagnose it. Most of the people who have it are not going to want to have anything to do with the doctor or psychiatrist who is trying to help them out and so they are going to ignore them and not take the help. Often it is going to take family members to see the issue and initiate the help that is needed before the person with the disorder is going to get the help. They are not going to go in on their own because they are not going to see that they have any issues at all.

Once you can get the person with the disorder to come into the door, the diagnosis of this disorder is going to be based on the assessment that is done in the clinic by a professional of mental health. The best way to do this is to present the different criteria of the disorder to the patient, these criteria are listed above, and ask them if they think that any of these describe them. This is going to get the participant involved in the cure, making it more likely to work. Plus, a doctor is usually not going to have enough time or outside experience with the patient to determine on their own if the characteristics are there and this can provide them with a usually truthful means of getting to it.

When you allow the person, who has this kind of disorder to actively help with the diagnosis, they are going to be more willing to get the help that the professional is going to get them. There are some clinicians though who decide that it is best to not tell their patients that they have this diagnosis because they believe that it is full of stigma and the person will be against the treatment because they may have heard in the past that this is an untreatable disorder. While this is one way to go, there is a lot of research to show that the person suffering from the disease should know about it to get the most effective treatment that is possible.

During this evaluation, the patient is going to be asked a lot of questions about their symptoms including when they began and how severe they were. The might also be asked some questions that relate to how these symptoms are impacting their life. Some of the issues that the doctor is going to take special notes about would be any thoughts that are about harming others, experiences with doing self-harm, and any thoughts of suicide that the person has.

The diagnosis is going to be based on what the patient has been reporting at sessions as well as what the doctor has been able to observe in their short time. These two things are usually going to be able to combine to give a good outlook on what is going on. There are a few other tests that can be done to help determine if borderline personality disorder is present in the person. Sometimes some laboratory tests or a physical exam are going to be done to help rule out some of the other things that might trigger these symptoms, such as the person abusing substances or a thyroid condition; both of which could cause some of the same behaviors as what is find in borderline personality disorder.

Once the disorder has been determined and diagnosed in a patient, it is time to get to work with giving them the treatment that they need to stay healthy and get their lives back. While this is going to be a lot of work and will take some time, it is something that must be done if the person wants to get their life back and be much happier. Here is some more information about how the disorder could be diagnosed and how the person should get the help that they need to start feeling better in no time.

International Classifications

There are a few classifications that you will be able to find that are used internationally to help make the diagnosis. These classifications can be nice because they allow the clinician to be able to do the diagnosis without having to go on their own personal beliefs and can keep everything organized and the same throughout. The idea of borderline personality disorder, is one that is recognized by the World Health Organization. It is then divided into two other categories which will be a bit below.

Impulsive Type

The first kind of category that is recognized in this is the impulsive type. Out of the things that are below, at least three of them need to be present to diagnose someone with this category of the disorder.

1. A marked tendency to get out of control or to act out. This is going to happen unexpectedly and will not be due to someone causing the issue or forcing them to act out. Often the act is going to be done by the person without them worrying or even thinking about the consequences that could happen with their action. This is just something that they are going to do, perhaps over a slight disagreement or other issue, that should not have been that big of a deal but which was turned into one.

2. A marked tendency of the sufferer to get into behavior that is considered quarrelsome and they are going to have a lot of conflicts with the others around them. This is especially going to be true with impulsive acts that have been criticized or thwarted. This is a person who is routinely getting into fights with others around them and who see any little slight as an excuse to get in a big fight together.

3. A liability to having strong outbursts when it comes to violence or anger. Not only are they having these issues, but they do not have the ability that is needed to control the explosions or other issues that come up. They will seem very angry but they will also seem like they do not have the means to come back down and be calm again even if they had wanted.

4. These people are also going to have some difficulty in staying with their course of action if they are not able to get a reward right away. They may have been really interested in doing it, but when it did not provide the immediate reward that they were looking for, they most likely became upset and angry and so decided to just give up on it. This is something that would happen quite often and the person would only stick with things they know they can finish and be rewarded with.

5. These people will often have capricious and unstable moods that can change almost without any warning. It might be hard to keep up with these kinds of people.

These are the five criteria that will often be found in someone who is dealing with the impulsive kind of this disorder. You are going to notice that they are going to do things often without any thought to what they are doing or what is going to happen when they are done, and this can be a dangerous thing. For a person to be diagnosed with this kind of disorder, they are going to need to have at least three of the things mentioned above present when they talk to their therapist in the office.

Borderline Type

Next comes the borderline type. This one is going to be a little bit different. This is going to take a bit from the list above and then adds in a bit from the list that is going to be presented below. You will need to have a minimum of three of those symptoms that are found for the impulsive type present as well as a minimum of 2 of the ones below to get a diagnosis of this category. Some of the things to look for include:

1. A person with this type would often have some uncertainty and disturbances in their self-image as well as their internal preferences and their aims in life. They do not think that they are worth much and even though they crave interaction with others, they are not sure why these others would want to have anything to do with them. They may wonder around a lot looking confused because they do not know who they are, what they should do with their lives, or what is to become of them.

2. They might also have a higher liability to get involved in relationships that are often unstable and intense. This might include those whirlwind relationships where they meet and get married in just a few short months, but it does not have to be this severe either to fit. Since the relationship is so unstable it is not going to last and since it was intense, it is likely to cause a sort of emotional crisis in the person who is suffering from the disorder.

3. These people are going to show really excessive efforts to never become abandoned. They are scared that one day they will wake up and not have anyone around to

be their friends or to help them out when they need. This is further complicated by the fact that they are pushing others away and are not very good at seeing other's points of view. They are going to work almost obsessively to make sure that others do not leave them alone so that they can always have the help and companionship that they are looking for.

4. They are also going to have frequent threats as well as acts of self-harm. This is often not in an attempt to get someone to act the way that they would like or to change the feelings of someone else. This is more of something that they do in the hopes of getting their own emotions in check. They are going to have a lot of trouble with their own emotions and since they are not able to keep them under control, they may turn to self-harm in the hopes of getting some relief.

5. Frequent feelings that surround them of emptiness. Because they do not have any plans for their future or for the things that they want to do in their lives, they are going to feel empty. They do not have any goals or long-term plans, so often they are just going to wander around and hope that things work out the best. This can lead to a life that is pretty empty.

6. They are going to often demonstrate behavior that is impulsive. This is going to include things such as substance abuse and speeding. The idea behind doing

these things is because it gives the sufferer a bit of a break for the bad feelings or uncontrolled emotions that they are going through so that they can just feel better for a bit. The issue comes when the person begins to feel a bit guilty about their behavior and so they will feel even worse than they did before.

As mentioned before, there needs to be quite a few things that are present before someone is going to be diagnosed with this form of the disorder. But those who meet these requirements should get the help that they need as soon as possible.

Millon's Subtypes

First we are going to take a look at the different subtypes that are used when it comes to borderline personality disorder. Theodore Millon has in the past proposed that there are four different subtypes when it comes to borderline personality disorder. Within these different categories, a person who has this disorder is going to exhibit usually one of more of the following things (these include the subtypes of the person with borderline personality disorder as well as the features that come with it):

- Discouraged—this subtype is also going to include the features of someone who is avoidant. You will find that a person who fits into this category is powerless, helpless, depressed, feels like there is no hope for them or their live, feels like they are in a constant jeopardy and vulnerable, humble, loyal, submissive, and pliant.

- Petulant—this category is also going to include the features of someone who is very negative about the thing that are going on around them. You will find that a person who fits into this category is quickly disillusioned and that they can be slighted at a moment's notice, resentful, pessimistic, sullen, defiant and really stubborn to get along with, restless, impatient, and very negative about everything.

- Impulsive—this category is also going to include the features of someone who is very antisocial and does not want to be around others. Some of the features that you will find in a person who suffers from this include someone who is potentially suicidal, someone who is irritable, gloomy, and can become agitated on occasion. These people are going to be fearful of losing things and are frenetic, distractible, flighty, superficial, and capricious.

- Self-destructive—this category is also going to include the features of someone is very masochistic or depressive. They are going to be really moody and high strung and these are going to show up more and more over time, they may think at times about suicide as an option are many of their positive features are going to begin to deteriorate. They are deferential, conforming, and angry over little things, and will turn inwards to themselves rather than making friends.

It is possible for someone to fit into more than one of these categories and have this kind of disorder, but this kind of helps to divide out the different symptoms and make them make a bit more sense for those who are learning about them or diagnosing them.

Family Members

Even the way that the person with the disorder is treating the others who are around them can be a way of diagnosing them. People who have this disorder are going to be much more prone to disliking their family members and they are often going to be angry at these same people. Often the person with the disorder is going to work to alienate themselves from the family because they are mad over some little slight or they are worried that the family members are going to become to see a problem. Often the family members are going to feel a bit helpless and angry about the way that they are relating with this person and may wonder what they can do to make things right again.

There was a study done in 2003 that found that the thoughts of the family members would change once they found out that the behavior was for a reason. In most cases, the anger and hurt towards the person with the disorder would go up once their family members began to understand what is going on. While this would not seem like something that would happen, it is often believed that these feelings are occurring because the family is being given the wrong kind of information about the disorder so they are blaming the person rather than the issue at hand.

The best way for family members to be able to help out the one that they love is to learn as much as possible about the disorder. It is easy to start looking through books and watching shows about the disorder and while this might be a good place to start in some cases, you will find that it is often the wrong information. Get out there and find the information that is the right information and this is going to help make more sense out of what you are seeing with your loved one.

This is going to be just as difficult for members of the family to handle as it is for the person who is going through the issue. They are the ones who have been emotionally harmed by their loved one not wanting to have anything to do with them. It is important that the family gets the therapy and help that they need to feel better about the situation. Understanding the whole situation and how it is affecting the family and the sufferer can make it easier to get through the whole situation together.

Adolescence

The onset of these symptoms of the disorder are usually going to happen sometime in adolescence or in young adulthood. In some cases, it is possible for the symptoms to occur in children, but this is not as prevalent. Symptoms that occur among a teenager is going to predict if borderline personality disorder is going to occur in their adult life. Some of the symptoms that can be present include severe shame, attempts to get in an exclusive relationship that often will not work out, self-injury that is not committing suicide, behavioral problems, being really sensitive to rejection, and severe issues with body image that go beyond what is normal for teenagers to feel.

It is discouraged to diagnose anyone who is younger than 18 with this disorder just because there are so many variables and mood changes in young adults and teenagers that it would be extremely easy to miss out or miss-diagnose someone who is just having their regular teenage concerns. This does not mean that the disorder cannot be diagnosed ahead of time, but it is usually dealt with in a case by case basis and most clinicians will not deal with at all until the person is 19. If it is diagnosed, the features will have to be present as well as consistent for a year or more before the diagnosis can be made.

If someone is diagnosed with this when they are a teenager, it is most likely going to predict that the person is going to have this same disorder when they are adults. Among those who were diagnosed with this disorder when they were younger, there is usually two groups; one is going to have the disorder and it is going to remain pretty stable over a period of time and then the other group that is going to have those who move in and also out of their diagnosis. An earlier diagnosis is sometimes helpful when trying to get an effective treatment plan in place, but since this kind of diagnosis is tricky, it is often not done. For those who are suffering from borderline personality disorder as teens, family therapy is usually the option that is the most preferred.

Chapter 3 Effective Treatments and Therapies for Borderline Personality Disorder

Borderline Personality disorder can be a scary condition- no one wants to be stuck with someone who is so unstable for the rest of their lives.

But you don't have to because it is not a permanent condition. Many people stick with the condition for longer than usual only because they couldn't identify that there is a problem and get a diagnosis early enough.

Once your loved one has been diagnosed, there are a lot of therapies and treatments that can help them improve and start to get better immediately.

Some of the effective treatments and therapies for Borderline Personality Disorder include:

Psychotherapy

Psychotherapy for Borderline Personality Disorder is also known as Talk Therapy. It involves the use of interpersonal or group interaction to try to change a person's behaviors and teach them better ways to interact with other people and handle the challenges they face with their moods, self-image, and thought process.

There are a lot of psychotherapy methods that are used to treat Borderline Personality Disorder but the most effective ones include:

☐ **Dialectal Behavior Therapy**

Dialectal Behavior Therapy also known as DBT, is a psychotherapy that helps to teach the patient healthy ways to cope with stress, manage conflicts, regulate their emotions, and improve their relationships.

It can also help to prevent destructive behaviors and eating disorders in people suffering from BPD.

Dialectal Behavior therapy was first introduced in the late 80's by Dr. Mashan Linehan, after discovering that Cognitive Behavioral Therapy(CBT), which commonly worked for people suffering from other personality disorders, was not effective for people suffering from Borderline Personality Disorder.

Dialectal Behavior Therapy is based on the concept of Dialectics, which is a belief that for every force, there is an opposing force that is stronger.

Patients are made to understand that:

- Change is inevitable and constant

- Everything is connected

- Opposing forces can come together to bring out positive results

People who suffer from BPD often have problems dealing with changes and opposing ideas, actions or personalities so this therapy teaches them how to embrace and manage changes, and help them to see that change is inevitable and an inherent quality of life itself.

Patients are also taught how to validate other people's opinions and ideas without necessarily accepting that it is the best approach.

Rather than throw tantrums because you said that Pizza is a better dinner than burger, they would be able to 'respect' your opposing ideas and opinions without necessarily accepting or adopting it.

Dialectal Behavior therapy is one of the most effective treatments for Borderline Personality Disorder and it is often done through group sessions, phone coaching and one on one therapy.

☐ **Schema-Focused Therapy (SCT)**

Schema-focused therapy helps patients to identify negative behaviors and patterns that they might have developed over time as a coping skill for Borderline Personality Disorder.

For instance, an adult who has suffered from BPD from when they were a child could have developed some negative traits like maybe binge-eating or snapping at people or being too clingy in order to prevent people from abandoning them.

Schema-focused therapy helps to identify these negative coping skills, and helps the patient to learn new, positive coping skills.

☐ Mentalization-based Therapy (MBT)

Another therapy that teaches BPD patients positive coping skills is Mentalization-based Therapy.

Patients are taught how to chart their own thoughts and feelings, and identify what they may be feeling at any point in time so that they can properly ponder on issues before reacting.

BPD patients are prone to impulsive habits and actions- they often react before they think unlike the rest of us who would often think about our actions and reactions carefully before letting them out.

Mentalization-based therapy basically helps patients to think and reflect on the consequences of their actions before acting them out.

☐ Transference-focused Psychotherapy (TFP)

Transference-focused psychotherapy is really great for BPD patients who are married or in romantic relationship, and want to improve their relationship with their partner.

The psychotherapist teaches the patient how to understand their emotions and develop good interpersonal relationship that the patient can duplicate with other people.

All of these therapies are effective and patients can choose one or a combination of therapies depending on what their problem areas are.

However, you would need the help of a mental healthcare professional or a psychologist to recommend the best therapy for the individual.

- Medications: Drugs like antidepressants, mood stabilizers, and antipsychotics are very helpful too especially for reducing symptoms like depression, anxiety, aggressiveness, and impulsiveness.

A doctor can prescribe medications to be used along with therapy because medications alone may only have temporary effects while a combination of both can provide permanent relief from Borderline Personality Disorder.

- Hospitalization: Hospitalization may be necessary where the patient may be suicidal or engaging in self-harm. They would have to be hospitalized and placed on suicide watch where they can start to take medications and therapies that would help to improve their condition.

- Self-help: There are a lot of ways that a person suffering from Borderline Personality Disorder can help themselves outside medications and therapies.

Some helpful self-help strategies include:

- Breathing Exercises: Breathing exercises help you calm down by sending signals to your sympathetic nervous system that is responsible for coordinating your flight or fight response.

Learning how to breathe, especially during distressful situations can help to prevent interpersonal conflicts.

Instead of responding impulsively, the patient can cultivate a habit of taking quick, deep breaths before responding to any situation.

It will not only help them calm down, but also help them ponder on actions before acting them out.

- Journaling and Mood-charting: The brain of a person with Borderline Personality Disorder can be likened to that of a little child. A little child is yet to understand why they are feeling a certain way, and they can't express their feelings so they would cry, throw tantrums and lash out all the time.

But if the child is able to identify what he or she is feeling at that moment, they can easily say "I'm hungry' rather than cry until you ask them if they want food.

Mood-charting can help a patient anticipate and identify their feelings at any point in time, so that they can avoid 'punishing' other people instead of looking inwards and tackling the issue from within them.

Mood-charting can be done with a pocket notebook, where the patient would have to record their moods and feelings at every hour of the day for a period of time, maybe a couple of weeks or months.

After some time, a pattern would emerge and it will be easy to tell how and what the patient may feel at different periods.

The patient would also be able to prepare themselves to handle the people and challenges that they are likely to come across during these periods.

- Family Therapy

The truth is that it is the family and friends that suffer most. If you are living with someone who suffers from BPD, it can take a negative toll on you and since the condition can be passed on to people who grew up or lived with BPD patients for a long time, your children may be at risk of developing Borderline Personality disorder too.

Family therapy is not only helpful for learning how to cope with, and live with patients without conflicts, it can also be a preventive or protective measure for people who have to live with or relate with a person who has the Borderline Personality Disorder.

Family therapy involves all members of the household working together with a therapist. You would all attend sessions as a group, where you would be taught how to communicate and cope with the patient, and how to avoid dangerous BPD family cycles from forming.

You would also be taught how to set boundaries and take care of yourself while caring for your loved one.

Family therapy is often more effective than individual therapy because the patient will still face difficulties at home if family and friends don't know how to communicate and live with them until their condition improves.

There are a lot of family therapy programs for Borderline Personality Disorder but a very common and effective one is Systems Training for Emotional Predictability and Problem-solving (STEPPS). It is a 20-week program that all family members have to attend. The program helps you learn how to predict the patient's reactions to common issues, and help you learn positive ways to respond, communicate and live with them.

Recovery Takes Time

Your loved one will get better as soon as they start receiving treatments but it is important to note that this will not happen overnight.

Some patients will get better almost immediately, while some might take years to respond to recovery so make sure you are patient with your loved one, and you give them as much time as they need to get better.

Chapter 4 Borderline Personality Disorder Myths Demystified

Borderline personality disorder is a disorder which was initially not accepted as a personality disorder. There are so many myths and misconceptions about it. There was no clarity about the disorder initially and so much confusion made it as a waste basket diagnosis. There was also a misconception that only women can have Borderline personality disorder which created much harm by not only keeping men unaware of the disorder but also putting women under too much of stress of having a disorder in them. There are very many Borderline personality disorder myths strewn across the internet apart from these. In this, we shall look at ten of the most common ones and demystify them.

Borderline personality disorder individuals are attention seekers

While it is true that some of the individuals suffering from Borderline personality disorder seek attention, it is important to note that not all of them are. Additionally, it is important to understand that Borderline personality disorder individuals seek attention to alleviate some of their negative feeling and emotions. They are looking for comfort in the attention in the hopes that the attention will deter them from self-harm.

Their behavior of suicide can get them responses from others but that is not an attention seeking method. It might look so, but it's not reality. They have the real urge to get out of this disorder as they are unable to cope up with it on a daily basis. Just to get free from the torture they undergo they do these acts which are often misread as attention seeking acts.

Borderline personality disorder individuals are manipulative

This is not true. People with Borderline personality disorder are not manipulative. To get a better understanding of this, think of everything that the person suffering from the disorder might have gone through. They might have suffered from abuse when they were younger or might be struggling with feeling of loss. Now, imagine yourself in the same shoes, what would you do to protect yourself? To what lengths would you go?

A person dealing with this disorder has so much of emotional imbalance that he seldom makes a sound decision, so his chances of manipulating others are almost minimal. As there is so much emotional imbalance, he is not able to manage situations and relationships. Being manipulative also depends on the mindset of the person who has Borderline personality disorder, like the suicide attempts can be just an attempt to communicate their pain and anxiety and not to influence others.

The behavior of the people having Borderline personality disorder is often misinterpreted as manipulative as their acts are just to maintain their small level of self-esteem and confidence.

Borderline personality disorder individuals are deceptive

This myth has links to the one about individuals with Borderline personality disorder being manipulative. This is because Borderline personality disorder individuals seem like convincing liars who set out to automatically mislead others. This is far from the truth. Persons suffering from Borderline personality disorder are very unlikely to do anything that will compound their feelings of loss and emptiness. Think about it. If you knew that performing a specific task would jeopardize your wellbeing, would you do it? In fact, research has shown that Borderline personality individuals find a lot of difficulty in lying.

There is a big difference between what we see and what reality is. Generally, there is a lot of unwanted information spread about the disorder based on the behavior of the patient which might always not be right.

Borderline personality disorder individuals are demanding

The reason why this is a very predominant myth is the fact that Borderline personality disorder takes a very long time to cure. How so? Think of suffering from a leg injury. With a leg injury, you are sure of the medication and the healing timeline. With Borderline personality disorder, it takes a long time, sometimes years/decades before you recognize the symptoms and move to the healing process. To the "normal" people, this can seem like a demanding personality because the person suffering from the ailment requires a lot of motivation and moral support.

Borderline personality disorder individuals are destructive

It is true that some Borderline personality disorder is very destructive. However, most Borderline personality disorders are not; well, perhaps not in the sense of outward destruction. As we had seen earlier, it is easy and common for a Borderline personality disorder to inflict pain upon them, impulsively rather than act out outward. This can manifest in reckless behavior such as unprotected sex, reckless driving and many more.

Borderline personality disorder individuals are obstructive

This is because Borderline personality disorder requires different approaches and thus, different treatment. Because the approach and medication is broad, the Borderline personality disorder individual might feel a bit like a guinea pig and thus reluctant to continue with some other form of experimental therapy or medication.

Borderline personality disorder individuals are dangerous

If you watch films depicting Borderline personality, they portray them as highly un-functional people with a lot of hate and destructive tendencies. This is so untrue. The truth is that Borderline personality disorder individuals will do everything in their power to avoid hurting people they care about, including harming themselves. Individuals suffering from Borderline personality disorder will sacrifice their own happiness if it means the happiness of those around him or her in the hopes that they are accepted and not rejected. The most danger a Borderline person poses is to him or herself. This characteristic distinguishes Borderline personality disorder from antisocial personality disorder.

BPD is untreatable

As we shall see later, on, you can use different methods to manage Borderline personality disorder. This is a recent change, because until recently, there was consensus that Borderline personality disorder is untreatable. However, this is wrong and treatments used prior to the understanding of the disorder contributed greatly to the misdiagnosis of the disorder and thus its ineffective treatment. Due to research, people suffering from Borderline personality disorder have a higher chance of recovery that people with Bipolar disorder. As long as someone can get access to proper treatment and therapy, there is no reason as to why they should not recover from Borderline personality disorder. Within two years from the treatment one can see a considerable relief in the symptoms of the patient. Research says that more than 85% of the people have got sustained relief. Once the treatment is completed fully, research says that 70-75% of the people don't meet the criteria of a Borderline personality disorder, later.

Borderline personality disorder individuals are uncooperative

There is some truth to this myth. However, let us look at this from the Borderline personality disorder point of view. How would you feel if someone treating you prejudiced you at every turn, labeled you names such as needy, difficult and time consuming; how would that make you feel? Would it make you cooperative? Persons suffering from Borderline personality disorder can sense these feeling in persons who are close to them and react accordingly by either withdrawing or harming himself or herself. At our best, it is hard to cooperate with people who we are not sure have our best interest at heart; this is often true for people suffering from Borderline personality disorder.

Borderline personality disorder individuals are non-compliant

This myth has links to the point above. The notion that a Borderline personality disorder individual is non-compliant is nowhere close to the truth. Part of the reason why this myth exists is the fact that a Borderline personality disorder individual under treatment by a psychologist or mental health individual with little understanding of the disorder will become unresponsive and hostile towards the treatment. It is just about creating artificial boundaries and not crossing them, imagining it will hurt badly if crossed.

Now that you know the truth from the myth it is time we move on to diagnosis and treatment of the disorder. The first step to diagnosis is recognition of the symptoms that we have already seen. If you have noticed any of the major symptoms and signs that we have looked at, here is how you go about preparing for your doctor's appointment and what to expect from your doctor.

Chapter 5 Diagnosis and Preparation for Your Doctor's Appointment

Diagnosis of Borderline personality disorder is one of the most difficult ones and is predominantly based on clinical valuation. Initially the dependability of the report is often questioned. There is so much overlapping of Borderline personality disorder with other disorders that it is uncertain whether the diagnosis systems takes into account all the possible factors. Though the trust and reliability on the diagnosis system has enhanced with better streamlining of the entire methods and better research in this regard.

Now standardized methods and techniques are followed to diagnose, more importance is given to observing a patient's behavior and listening to their explanation about what they are undergoing in life, relation etc.

A better diagnosis strategy is to involve the patients in the entire thing so that they actively participate and take efforts for the improvement of the same. In some cases, though, the patient is kept unaware of the disorder to save them from shock and further depression. In most cases, it appears as though patients with knowledge of their disorder have a better improvement rate and cooperate better for the treatment.

The diagnostic and statistical manual states that a person has to meet a minimum of 5 and a maximum of 9 symptoms to be diagnosed with Borderline personality disorder, with the main symptoms being unstable relationships, impulsive behavior, a negative self-image etc. Diagnostic and statistical manuals state alternate methods to diagnose Borderline personality disorder include another set of 6-7 criteria to be met by the patient. However, it had become highly uncertain to come to a conclusion using these criteria as they were widely defined.

Later, for clarification and easy understanding, the various criteria were grouped into five categories i.e. emotions, self-sense, interpersonal relationships, cognition and behavior.

However, the diagnosis of Borderline personality disorder is mostly done wrong. Either Borderline personality disorder is underestimated or overestimated. The intensity/stage of Borderline personality disorder can be found with the impact with which they emotionally respond to the interrogation and questioning. High vulnerability of emotion suggests that the patient is at an extreme level of Borderline personality disorder, whereas, the patient who is low on emotion is supposed to have less intense stage of Borderline personality disorder.

There are various methods that a practitioner can take up to diagnose Borderline personality disorder:

After recognizing the patterns of the disorder, what do you do next? Where do you go from there? The most critical thing now is seeking medical attention. In the initial stages, your doctor (if he is a GP) may recommend you to a psychiatrist or mental health physician. However, before we get to that part, here is what you can do to prepare for your appointment.

How to prepare for your doctor's appointment

Before meeting your doctor, here is what you can do (remember that even though self-diagnosis is frowned upon, that is where diagnosis starts):

1. If you notice any of the symptoms we have seen, write them done before going for your doctor's appointment. Additionally, you should note down any of the symptoms in other family members with the same tendencies. This will help you ensure that the doctor gets a proper background into your condition.

2. In addition to writing down the symptoms you exhibit, there is also need to write down key personal information such as mental or physical trauma experienced in the past and current major stresses.

3. Making a list of all your pre-existing medical conditions is important. You should supply your doctor with a list of all medications you are taking at that particular moment.

4. Moral support is the key in the diagnostic stage of the ailment. Therefore, you should aim to take a friend or a family member along with you to your doctor's appointment. This is important because someone who has known you for a long time may notice things

about you that you do not notice. In turn, the friend (or family member) will provide your GP or physician with important information that could help in your diagnosis.

5. Additionally, you should do a lot of research into the disorder and write down a list of questions that you would like to ask your doctor. This will assist you and your doctor to make the best out of the appointment.

You should ask some common questions such as:

- *What is the cause of the condition or symptoms and are there any other possible causes of the symptoms?

- *What are the most likely treatments for my condition?

- *After treatment, at what level can I expect my symptoms to improve?

- *How long will be the treatment last and how frequent will be the therapy sessions?

- *What medications should I expect to take?

- *Do the medications have any side-effects?

- *Do I need to follow any precautionary measures or restrictions?

- *If I have preexisting conditions, how best can I manage them together with this condition?

- *What role do my family members and friends play in my rehabilitation?

- *Where can I access printed materials, or which websites should I visit to get more information?

While formulating your list of question, do not restrict yourself. Ask as many questions as you need to get all the information you require to better understand the condition.

What to expect from your doctor?

In addition to preparing yourself mentally and physically, here is a list of some of the thing you should expect from your doctor. These include questions and then other things.

- *Which symptoms do you exhibit? (This is why you must write down which symptoms you exhibit)

- *At which point did you notice these symptoms?

- *What effects do these symptoms have on your relationships? Both personal and work related?

- *How often do you experience mood swings in a particular day?

- *How often do you experience feelings of betrayal?

- *Are you capable of managing your anger?

- *Are you comfortable with being alone?

- *Do you get bored easily?

- *How would you describe your sense of self-worth?

- *Do you experience feelings of being evil or bad? How often?

- *Do you have problems with risky or self-destructive behavior?

- *Do you think of committing suicide or have you ever tried to commit suicide?

- *Do you abuse drugs such as alcohol, illegal drugs and how often do you use them?

- *Which words would you use to describe your childhood and early life? (This is inclusive of the relationship with your parents)

- *Did you experience mental or physical abuse as a child?

- *Are you or any of your close family members suffering from or ever been diagnosed with any mental disorder?

- *Do you have any prior mental health problems? What was the diagnosis of this mental disorder and what medication are you using?

- *Do you have any other medical condition that is currently under treatment right now?

Here are some things you can do if you are suffering from the disorder and have suicidal thoughts.

- *Call your local emergency services immediately.

- *Get in touch with your local suicide hotline number. This is very helpful because at the other end of the hotline are qualified counselors.

- *Call a specialist. In this case, you can call your health care provider, health specialist, or doctor.

- *Talk to a supportive friend, trusted peer, loved one, or co-worker. This is to give you support.

- *Get in touch with someone from your local community.

Diagnosis and Test

Borderline personality disorder diagnosis entails:

- *An interview with a trained physician (mental health expert) or doctor

- *A psychological evaluation

- *A clinical history

- *Symptoms and signs

The diagnosis of the disorder must meet the criteria spelled out in DSM (diagnostic and statistical manual of mental disorder). The manual is updated and published by the APA (American

Psychiatric Association). This manual is widely used by the mental health experts and medical insurance companies. The manual states that for someone to qualify for a Borderline personality disorder diagnosis, they must exhibit the following signs and symptoms:

#-An intense fear of being alone (abandonment)

#-Display a pattern of unstable relationships

#-Display impulsive or self-destructive behavior

#-Show a history of self-injury or suicidal thoughts

#-Consistent mood swings

#-Chronic emptiness and loneliness

#-Temper. This can manifest in bouts of anger that may result in physical fights

#- Brief but intense periods of paranoia.

As we had seen earlier, Borderline personality disorder is predominant in adults. This is because as the child grows, signs and symptoms that appear to relate to Borderline personality disorder tend to go away as the child matures. This could loosely be taken to mean that Borderline personality disorder arises when the signs and symptoms don't go away even as someone enters into adulthood.

Chapter 6 Inner Therapy

Anger

As codependents, we have been taught to suppress our anger and were even punished for displays of anger as a child. When our parents would get angry at us and we displayed any anger in return, we were scolded for doing so and immediately punished.

When one of our parents displayed rage or angry outbursts, we subconsciously told ourselves that we would never follow in their footsteps, that we would do anything possible to not be like them. It should come as no surprise then that we often withhold our anger in an attempt to be nice and show that we are not like our parents.

Unfortunately, this typically leads to unexpected outbursts when we can no longer hold it in. You might have snapped at your ex for a seemingly meaningless reason, yet they are unaware that the anger has been building inside of you all along. Rather than releasing it all at once and letting it out in a healthy, constructive manner, you resort to bottling it up inside until you can no longer hold it in.

Have you ever noticed how your behavior drastically changes around your parents? Do you often become irritated with everything one or both of them do? This is primarily due to unresolved childhood rage that is sitting within you.

If you find yourself waking up in the middle of the night, unable to go back to bed, you are likely dealing with unresolved anger. From this point on, you are not going to resist or fear your anger. Anger is an essential and healthy emotion that was biologically gifted upon us. If it was so harmful to us, then we wouldn't have evolutionarily adapted to feel it.

This does not mean that I want you to publicly display your anger and purposefully become an angry person! Quite the opposite. I have listed three healthy methods below for releasing your anger. Once you incorporate these methods, you will start noticing how much more at ease you feel on a daily basis. You will no longer feel the need to sporadically display your anger, often towards those who have nothing to do with it.

Doing this was groundbreaking for me!

These tools might very well feel unnatural for most of you. That is ok. In order for these tools to be fully effective, you must follow them precisely as I specified above. For instance, do not use one hand instead of two while hitting your bed with the bat.

Online/Mobile Dating Apps - Stay Away

Here are the top five reasons why I am not using online or mobile dating apps:

We live in an age of instant gratification. One where we can order items from Amazon and have them arrive at our door within two days, send each other money within seconds and feel good about ourselves when we rack up 100+ likes for a Facebook profile picture within a few hours.

A low-commitment hookup culture is emerging and many people I know are cycling through partners, still looking to find someone whom they are compatible with.

Take what you will from this list. I believe that we as humans share the same desires and wants deep down inside. We subconsciously strive for the same things – intimacy, connection and love.

1. Life is About Delayed Gratification – After reflecting upon the periods when I was feeling good about myself and the direction of my life, the overarching theme throughout these times was that I wasn't looking for instant gratification. I knew that things would unfold as they were meant to with due time. As a male in my late 20's, I have been through my fair share of ups and downs. However, reaching for Tinder is nearly as bad as reaching for the bottle. You really want someone else to accept you because you are struggling accepting yourself.

2. To Face Reality - As a society, it seems that we are shifting towards a state of emotional intolerance. We are unable to sit with our emotions and are constantly seeking the highs and avoiding the lows at any cost. Tinder serves as a band-aid for the soul. Emotional growth and a true sense of self comes from being comfortable with our feelings of boredom, despair and pain.

Those feelings won't annihilate us. If anything, they will teach us that we can feel negative emotions and grow from them.

3. To Achieve My Goals - While I was only using online dating apps for a week, when I was matching with attractive women, I started to feel a false sense of accomplishment. This almost immediately lowered my desire to pursue my true goals in life. Feeling accepted by the opposite sex biologically elicits a sense of complacency. My goals don't entail holding down a 9-5 or leading the commercialized lifestyle that the media or big business crafted for us.

4. To Meet The Right Girl – My vision of a suitable partner has shifted over time. I used to follow my natural tendency to pursue someone who mimics my Mom, as I was naturally attracted to that. Unfortunately, those traits are not ones that will enable me to lead a healthy relationship. My partner should have a strong self of self and be able to facilitate a nourishing and loving relationship. We should complement each other, yet not need each other.

5. To Find Real Intimacy – Like many men today, I once thought that hooking up with a new girl every week was exciting and proof of my value to myself and others. Avoiding commitment really means that you are afraid to share your true self with someone else. I have been there and I can look back on those times when I subconsciously sabotaged a relationship that could have thrived because of my fear to be vulnerable. Once again, this comes back to not being comfortable with who you are deep

down inside. While I am not starving for someone to share my life with, I desire to find someone that I can expose myself to and build a meaningful relationship with. Tinder will doubtfully supply me with that person.

Recognition List Tool

Continuing on the path towards building your core strength is an ongoing activity, one that requires continuous effort. Eventually, you will find yourself. The following tool nicely supplements the strength building tool from week 2.

Chapter 7 Treatment and Medication

Each person's experience with borderline personality disorder is different. Some symptoms may be more dominant; while for one he could be more paranoid, for another he would be more dissociative. Depending on the situation and circumstances, a therapist can recommend the right treatment for borderline personality disorder.

In addition, it may be tempting for some people with BPD to attempt managing the disorder without resorting to therapy. In order to fully recover from the symptoms, one must be able to learn coping skills that they need to manage BPD every day. The urge to manage BPD without professional therapeutic help may have stemmed from negative experiences with doctors and therapists in the past. But without the commitment to recover fully from borderline personality disorder, the chances of overcoming the symptoms are highly unlikely without the guidance of therapy.

Therapy teaches important life skills that are needed by people who suffer from BPD, if they want to enjoy living a normal life again. These life skills are also crucial if the patient wants to enjoy a quality life. There are many resources on how one can self-help to reduce symptoms of BPD, but without the guidance of a licensed professional who is dedicated to helping you manage your disorder, you will never have an objective understanding or know if you have actually recovered from your illness.

The recovery process can be difficult alone, which is why this book discusses how family, friends, and loved ones can provide actual support. The moral support lent by loved ones will be valuable in recovery. Additionally, because borderline personality disorder is an actual mental condition, it is not advisable to go about it without professional intervention. If BPD is left untreated it can lead to serious consequences on oneself and to loved ones.

When one has BPD it can oftentimes be a scary experience that leaves one feeling isolated because it causes a strain on relationships. Individuals with BPD need the guidance of therapists to overcome this aspect of the disorder so that they can go back to their normal life and benefit from the joy that healthy human relationships can bring. Treatment for BPD can provide people with valuable skills that they need to carry out into the world for maintaining interpersonal relationships. Additionally, treatment can reduce the stress involved through the prescription of medication that decreases BPD symptoms.

Psychotherapy

Psychotherapy is the most common treatment of choice for people with mental illnesses especially those who have BPD. Although there are many forms of psychotherapy, they all have one goal in common and that is to help patients better understand the way their thoughts and emotions operate. It is an important aspect of treatment because while medication can help reduce certain symptoms of borderline personality disorder, it will not teach patients how to learn coping skills or regulate emotions the way psychotherapy does.

Psychotherapy is also crucial in helping people refrain from committing suicide. This is why therapists and other medical professionals involved stay in touch with the patient, constantly evaluating their vulnerability to suicide throughout the entire treatment. When a patient has severe feelings of suicide, hospitalization is the next step.

Dialectical Behavior Therapy

The most famous and effective form of psychotherapy known today is Dialectical Behavior Therapy or DBT. It was founded by Marsha Linehan, and is a program that teaches people how to take better control of their lives and emotions. DBT also has a strong focus on emotion regulation, self-knowledge, and cognitive restructuring. DBT has a comprehensive approach and is usually conducted with a group. However, the skill set taught through Dialectical Behavior Therapy is considered complex and therefore not recommended to people who have difficulty learning new concepts.

Dialectical Behavior Therapy utilizes two concepts: validation and dialectics. In validation, the client is taught to accept that their emotions are real, acceptable, and valid. On the other hand, dialectics is a form of philosophy which teaches that life is not to be seen as black and white. It also reinforces the importance of accepting ideas even though they are contradicting to one's own beliefs.

The primary goal of DBT is to help the client break their notions of the world and enjoy freedom from living a rigid life that causes one to resort to self-destructive behavior. DBT is held in weekly group as well as individual sessions. Clients are given a number that they can call any time if they feel that their symptoms are getting worse and need emergency assistance. In order for DBT to be effective, teamwork is expected. Clients need to work closely with their therapists as well as the other people met during group sessions.

While Dialectical Behavior Therapy is generally the most successful form of treating BPD, it has shown to be particularly useful in treating those who are more prone to suicide. Individuals with BPD resort to suicide because they feel that they have lost absolutely all control in life and suicide is the only thing they can do that can help them. Dialectical Behavior Therapy is particularly effective in helping people regain a sense of control in their lives. Once DBT has helped a patient be in control, therapists can focus on other aspects of their life to improve.

Therapists specializing in DBT work with those who are prone to suicide by engaging them in mindfulness, interpersonal effectiveness, emotion regulation, and distress tolerance. When people with BPD learn that there are healthy ways of coping and handling one's emotions, the risk of them committing self-harm and suicide are significantly decreased.

Borderline personality disorder, just like other personality disorders, is challenging to treat. Because the goal of treatment is to change the way a person views the world, stress, and other people, treatment is usually lengthy. Treatment for BPD is usually at least a year but can go on for much longer.

There are also other forms of psychotherapy that are used to address borderline personality disorder that focus on conflict resolution and social learning theory. These are more solution-focused therapies which fail to address the core issue of people who suffer from BPD which is difficulty regulating their emotions.

Schema Focused Therapy

Schema Focused Therapy is a type of psychotherapy whose primary goal is to identify and treat unhealthy ways of thinking. Some elements of schema focused therapy include elements that are also found in cognitive behavioral therapy (CBT) and combines it with other methods of psychotherapy.

Schema focused therapy is founded on the principle that if a person's basic childhood needs such as love, acceptance, and a desire for safety are inadequate, this results in the development of unhealthy ways of thinking about the world. These are referred to as maladaptive early schemas. Schemes are defined as broad patterns of behavior and thinking. They are more than simply beliefs because they are closely held patterns that affect the way one perceives and interacts with the world.

The schema theory suggests that schemas occur when events in one's present life bear a resemblance to events in the past that are directly related to the creation of the schema. When a person has unhealthy schemas as a result of a difficult childhood, they will end up developing unhealthy ways of thinking as a response to the situation. Furthermore, schema theory suggests that the symptoms of borderline personality disorder are usually caused by a difficult childhood wherein a child may have experienced abandonment, trauma, or maltreatment by one or both parents, resulting to the development of maladaptive early schemas.

Schema focused therapy for borderline personality disorder seeks to identify relevant schemas in a person's life, and tie them to schemas present in past events. A therapist works to help the patient process the emotional response that arise due to the schema. They then work on addressing unhealthy coping methods to help the patient respond to the scheme in a healthy manner. Schema focused therapy may involve exercises that are designed to halt unhealthy behavioral patterns, change the way one thinks, and encouraging the patient to vent out their anger.

Transference Focused Therapy

Transference Focused Therapy utilizes the patient-therapist relationship in order to improve how a person with borderline personality disorder sees the world. Transference is defined as the process wherein emotions are transferred from one person to the other. It is a key principle used in psychodynamic therapies where it is suggested that the way a client feels about persons that are important in their lives are transferred to his therapist. Through transference therapy, the therapist can clearly understand how the patient interacts with the people in his life in order to help them learn to effectively manage relationships. Eventually, the goal of transference focused therapy is to help patients enjoy having stable relationships again.

Therapists of transference focused therapy believe that symptoms of borderline personality disorder that arise from dysfunctional relationships one experienced during childhood continue in adulthood, thereby damaging the ability of these adults to have normal, healthy relationships. The interactions we have with our primary caregivers during childhood contributes to how we develop a sense of self and also affects how we perceive other people. If one does not have a healthy relationship with their caregivers during childhood, this results in adults having difficulty relating to other people and having a good sense of oneself.

Evidence shows that maltreatment or trauma or loss of caregivers during childhood increases one's risk in developing borderline personality disorder. And because these symptoms have a negative impact, preventing one from developing relationships with people later on, some experts on BPD agree that it is important to address this by helping people focus on improving relationships through transference focused therapy.

With this kind of therapy there is a focus on the relationship between the patient and the therapist. Unlike other forms of therapy where the therapist provides instructions on what the patient should do, transference focused therapy involves asking the client numerous questions during the discussion while they explore reactions. Furthermore, there is added emphasis on events that happen in the present moment instead of seeking out past experiences. For example, instead of spending time discussing issues with caregivers during one's childhood, the discussion is focused on how the client relates to their own therapist.

Therapists who practice transference based therapy are also skilled at remaining neutral, which is a reason why this kind of treatment is effective. They know not to give their opinion on their patient's reaction, and will also not be available outside session hours except for emergencies.

Mentalization-Based Therapy

Mentalization-based therapy (MBT) is another form of psychotherapy. MBT is based on the premise that people who have borderline personality disorder have difficulty thinking about their own thoughts. This means that people with BPD are unable to examine their own thoughts, beliefs, opinions, and if they are realistic and useful to them. An example of this is when individuals with BPD may have sudden urges to harm themselves and end up giving in without thinking about the consequences of their actions.

MBT is also important because it helps people realize that others have their own thoughts and beliefs, and your own interpretation of their mental states is not always correct. Additionally, it helps people realize that actions will have an impact on other people's mentality. The main goal of MBT is to help clients recognize their own as well as others' mental states. It also teaches people with BPD how to step back from their own thoughts and examine if they are valid first. MBT may be conducted within a hospital as a form of inpatient therapy. Treatment is composed of daily sessions with a therapist as well as group sessions.

MBT usually lasts around 18 months, but depending on the need some patients may be asked to be an inpatient for the entire duration of their treatment. Some hospitals and treatment facilities will allow patients to leave at specified times during the course of their treatment.

Therapeutic Communities

Therapeutic Communities (TC) is a form of psychotherapy wherein people with various psychological conditions interact in a structured environment. This kind of treatment is best suited for those who have issues dealing with emotions and who are suicidal. By teaching them the skills needed for healthy social interaction with a wide range of people, people with borderline personality disorder can better cope with their problems. TC therapy is usually residential and held in houses where clients stay 1-4 days a week.

Apart from individual and group sessions involved in TC, it also requires patients to participate in other activities designed to improve one's social skills and boost confidence. These activities include doing household chores, prepare and cook meals, play games, and participate in recreational activities. Therapeutic communities also involve all participants in regular community meetings where people with different psychological conditions meet in order to discuss issues and concerns within the community.

One of the unique features of the therapeutic community method of treatment is that it is run democratically. All members, including staff, can contribute their opinion on how TC's should be run. In fact, they can even vote if they think an individual should or shouldn't be admitted within the community. This means that even if one's therapist thinks that a therapeutic community is the best form of treatment for a case of borderline personality disorder, it doesn't mean that they will automatically be granted entry. Guidelines for acceptable behavior are defined in each TC because they set restrictions such as the prohibition of alcohol consumption, violence towards one self and other members of the community. Members who break the guidelines may be asked to leave the TC.

Although a therapeutic community is one of the widely accepted methods of treatment for people with borderline personality disorder, there is insufficient evidence to tell if a TC is effective for everyone. This is particularly the case for people with BPD who have difficulty following rules since TC's can be quite strict with guidelines.

Self-Care

Over the course of treatment, patients are usually given a telephone number that they can call if they think they are undergoing a severe crisis. It could occur when people with BPD are experiencing episodes of extreme symptoms and are more prone to self-harm and suicide. A number may be directed to the community mental health care practitioners, social workers, or other medical professionals. Depending on the area, a crisis resolution team service may also be available since they specialize in caring for people with serious mental health issues. Oftentimes these teams come to the rescue of individuals who may require hospitalization because of suicide attempts.

Those who suffer from borderline personality disorder usually find that merely talking to someone about what they are going through can help them get out of their crisis. Certain cases, although rare, may require medication such as tranquilizers to calm one's mood. Medications such as these are usually prescribed for 7 days to stabilize emotions.

Individuals with borderline personality disorder are encouraged to attend support groups for social support from those who are going through the same experience as they are. Support groups are useful in providing moral support through sharing common thoughts and feelings. Patients can also try coping skills and learn how to regulate their emotions with friends they make at these support groups. They have proven to be a crucial part of helping people with BPD expand their skill set while developing healthy social relationships and eventually reduce their symptoms in the long run.

If you are the one suffering from borderline personality disorder, you may also find it challenging to take better care of yourself. However, those who are diagnosed with BPD should make it a priority to take better care of themselves because the symptoms may be exacerbated when one neglects self-care.

The basics of self-care involve engaging in activities that promote relaxation and good health. This means getting enough exercise, good sleep, taking the medications as prescribed by your therapist, eating nutritious food, and dealing with stress in healthy ways. People who take good care of themselves are less prone to suffering from psychiatric illnesses which is why self-care is necessary for everyone. It is especially important in those who are suffering from BPD because while it can not only worsen the symptoms, it can also result in slower recovery.

Many people tend to underestimate the importance of good sleep when it comes to proper self-care. If a person with BPD does not get adequate sleep they can become more anxious, irate, and aggressive. Here are some tips to help you get better sleep:

1. Avoid alcohol, nicotine, and caffeine a few hours before your bedtime. However, you will be able to sleep better if you completely eradicate these factors from your lifestyle.

2. Do not eat large meals before bedtime because it could cause upset stomach. Try to eat a light, filling meal at least three hours before you intend to go to sleep. On the other hand, don't go to bed with an empty stomach because a growling stomach caused by hunger can wake you up in the middle of the night and interfere with your sleep patterns. A warm glass of milk or a light snack are healthier alternatives.

3. Create a pre-bedtime ritual that will help you relax and soothe your mind. Some of these may include reading, aromatherapy, or taking a warm bath.

4. Establish a regular sleeping schedule which means avoiding naps, waking up at the same time each day, and sleeping at the same time every night.

5. Ensure that your bedroom is conducive to proper sleep. Lights should be turned off and noises reduced as much as possible. The temperature should also be just right.

People with borderline personality disorder should also pay close attention to diet and nutrition. Symptoms and moods can easily be affected by overeating, skipping meals, and eating food that have no nutritional value. Take supplements if needed, avoid fatty food, and make sure that you get a lot of fruits and vegetables in each day.

Exercise also has an impact on mental health, this is why more doctors recommend their patients to live an active lifestyle. In addition, regular workouts increase the release of endorphins in the body, which help you feel more elated. Exercise works for the person with BPD by providing a healthy outlet for stress and stabilizing one's mood. Setting fitness goals for yourself and achieving them will also boost self-esteem and confidence.

People who already suffer from BPD are less likely to take good care of their health and suffer from other disorders that arise from a sedentary and unhealthy lifestyle later on. These include arthritis, obesity, high blood pressure, chronic fatigue syndrome, back pain, and urinary incontinence. Those who suffer from BPD are known to have unhealthy lifestyles: smoking cigarettes, consumption of alcohol, lack of exercise and proper sleep, and a dependency on pain medication. The symptoms of borderline personality disorder causes people to make poorer lifestyle choices because of stressful events or genetics, which will cause serious health problems down the line. Furthermore, the link between one's physical health and borderline personality disorder can be complex although more research is being conducted on it.

Given these facts, there are still many things you can do to improve the state of your health. Pay close attention to unhealthy habits that you can change today, such as quitting smoking and reducing your alcohol intake. Studies have shown that people who were once diagnosed with BPD and who recovered successfully no longer report health issues. Getting treatment for BPD can significantly reduce your chances of developing physical ailments and creating good habits.

Medications are another important aspect of self-care for people with BPD. While many people think that medication does not constitute self-care, those who are not committed to taking their medications regularly or take the incorrect doses may only exacerbate their symptoms and slow down recovery time. Avoid making changes to your medication without consulting your physician. On a similar note, not taking your medication at all is unhealthy and can have dangerous side effects.

Managing stress properly is also part of self-care. The presence of stress may be inevitable in our daily lives, and it does not mean that it is automatically a negative element. The key here is to learn how to manage stress effectively. Sometimes, stress may feel overwhelming and during these times you may need additional help to overcome them.

Medication

Some doctors agree that medication is useful in the treatment of people with borderline personality disorder but others disagree. Today, there is still no medication that is licensed for the treatment of BPD. However, some forms of medicine have proven useful in reducing symptoms in certain people.

Usually, selective serotonin reuptake inhibitors (SSRI) are by default the first kind of medication that is prescribed to patients. SSRI's are designed to reduce impulsivity, depression, anger, suicidal behavior, and anxiety in people who suffer from mental health problems.

Medications such as anti-depressants and anti-anxiety pills may be useful to reduce symptoms especially during a crisis or emergency. The most common kinds of antidepressants prescribed for patients of borderline personality disorder include Prozac, Zoloft, Nardil, Wellbutrin, and Effexor. However, this kind of medication is not encouraged for long-term use particularly because depression and anxiety are often short-term symptoms that may come and go as a result of various stressors in a person's life.

Antipsychotics also have a positive effect on patients even though they don't suffer from BPD. These are effective in reducing paranoia, anxiety, hostility, anger, as well as impulsivity in people with borderline personality disorder. Common antipsychotic medications include Haldol, Clozaril, Risperdal, Seroquel, and Zyprexa.

Mood stabilizers are another form of medication that is used to treat symptoms of borderline personality disorder. These are effective in treating impulsivity, mood swings, and the intense changes in emotions caused by BPD. Common types of mood stabilizers include Lithobid, Depakote, Tegretol, and Lamictal.

Medication that specializes in reducing anxiety are known as anxiolytics, and are also prescribed for BPD. While anxiolytics are given to patients of borderline personality disorder, there is still insufficient evidence on the effectiveness of these medications in treating BPD as a whole. In fact, there have been cases where certain types of anxiolytics, known as benzodiazepines, were shown to increase the symptoms of BPD in other people. Common types of anxiolytics used for BPD patients include Valium, Xanax, Ativan, Klonopin, and Buspar.

Studies are currently being done to test the effectiveness of other types of medication for borderline personality disorder. Findings from some studies have shown that taking supplements such as omega 3 fatty acids can reduce feelings of hostility and aggression in those suffering from BPD.

People with borderline personality disorder also need to be consistent in taking the medication as prescribed by their doctor. Honesty is also crucial in the success of medication for treating BPD. If you are taking care of someone, you may encourage this by reminding them to be open about their medication, what they feel, if they missed taking it, and other concerns they might have about it.

Before accepting medications from a physician, it is necessary to discuss any side effects thoroughly. If the side effects seem harmful, other forms of medicine may be considered especially if it is clear that the side effects are greater than the benefits. Medication used for borderline personality disorder may vary depending on the kind of medicine. Some of the common side effects are detailed below:

Antidepressants:

- Headache

- Insomnia

- Reduced appetite

- Sedation

- Sexual dysfunction

- Weight gain

Mood stabilizers:

- Acne

- Tremors

- Weight gain

- Gastrointestinal distress

Antipsychotics:

- Akathisia

- Dry mouth

- Weight gain

- Sexual dysfunction

- Sedation

Anti-anxiety:

- Fatigue

- Sleepiness

- Mental slowness

- Memory problems

- Impaired coordination

How To Know If A Medication Is Working

When you start to take medication for borderline personality disorder, this will result in both emotional and physical changes. If a medication is working well, the first thing that you may notice is a positive change in the way you respond to situations. Although the change is usually gradual and subtle, people experience the benefits of medications in a different time frame from other people. In fact, the positive changes are usually not felt unless they have been happening for some time. It is also common for other people to notice the changes in your emotional response before you do, so you may want to ask people that you are usually with if they notice any changes.

These are other indications to help you recognize when a medication is effective for you:

1. You no longer think about certain events or issues with the same frequency as before. Your pattern of thoughts is no longer inconsistent and no longer wanders from one subject to another. Although you may experience some fatigue when you begin treatment, there is a noticeable improvement on clarity and focus. It will also be easier to focus on one thought for a longer period of time.

2. Things, places, events, or people that used to be triggers no longer have the same effect on you. There will also be sudden improvements in communicating better with other people.

3. When you face situations that used to give you anxiety, you now face it with a sense of calmness. However, if you are taking benzodiazepines it is recommended to talk to your physician about this change in response.

4. Things that used to upset or anger you no longer elicits the same response.

Gender-Specific Treatment

Borderline personality disorder treatments focused on women are available to help them cope better because the way men and women manage their emotions when dealing with the illness will differ. This is why some patients prefer gender-specific treatment options. However, not all centers will have women-only treatment options available.

Each person's BPD case is as unique as their thumbprint. The important aspect of treatment is to find qualified professionals who can design a program that will be most effective for your individual needs and who may adapt as you start to recover from the illness.

Women who have borderline personality disorder are also at higher risk for developing co-occurring disorders such as eating disorders, anxiety, suicide, and depression. If you are experiencing these, it is necessary to find treatment that will also address co-occurring disorders.

Chapter 8 Psychodynamic theory

Despite the fact that the psychodynamic approaches are diverse, the truth is that they contribute to explanatory and descriptive frameworks encompassing both pathological and normal behaviors of the disorder. It is these kinds of frameworks that address the personality structures, beliefs, and motivation and the conflicts linked with the disorder.

It is important to note that there are three main psychodynamic constructs that are interrelated and are relevant to the description and understanding of personality disorders namely;

– Ego strength

– Defense style

– Mental representation of others and self

The ego strength simply refers to the extent to which ego carries out reality testing functions and effectively deals with impulses. This developed through experience especially when one is in the context of a relationship.

Defense style, on the other hand, refers to the characteristic ways of anxiety management and coping with the external threats. It exists within the continuum of both primitive defense and mature defense styles.

The mental representation of others and self refers to an instance where a child during their early days tries to internalize their mental representation of self and their loved ones. It is these kinds of introjects that are charged internal objects responsible for effectively shaping the response to stress and threats.

When these internalized introjects are harmful and conflicting, there is a high likelihood that an individual will experience difficulty having effective control and relating with others. In other words, psychodynamic perspectives contribute a great deal to the understanding of the core BPD deficits that revolve around object-relations, identity, and dysregulation of emotions. this is the case as relates to motivation processes, conflicts, personality organizations, affects and defenses.

The approach goes a long way in gaining deeper insight into the personality of an individual, determining whether it is healthy or not so that it offers an integrative account that deals with motivation and affects and how they relate to cognition. Such an approach permits one to formulate specific questions that will help people with BPD to determine;

–   What their desires, beliefs, conflicts and fears are

–   What their coping resources are for dealing with conflicts and effects

–   What their object-relations are – both internally and externally along with their self-concept

In terms of addressing these questions, the psychodynamic framework perceives development of psychopathology in a relational context as well as the attachment needs of an individual. What you need to note about attachment processes is that they appear specifically relevant to the understanding of BPD. There are lots of research information available that indicates development of attachment for both intra- and interpersonal functioning as well as ensuing defenses and conflicts that come up when the attachment needs are not met adequately.

What is interesting is that there are several people who believe that BPD is often a result of caregiving styles that are linked with the severe insecurity as well as disorganized attachments. Note that disorganized attachments are linked with the approach-avoidance conflict, in which caregiving is considered both a source of threat and security.

It is this form of conflict that creates an intolerable situation in which a child is not able to develop consistent behavioral and affective response patterns to threats. Neither are they able to rely on internal beliefs of comforting caregivers whenever they are distressed or frustrated.

The immature defensive maneuvers handling projections, dissociations and splits often causes a distortion in the child's understanding of relationships with self and others. While this is not entirely static, you must bear in mind that childhood attachment patterns often persist throughout life and a person with BPD often manifests these conflicts and fears.

In so many ways, the psychodynamic approach is viewed as a complementary approach to BPD rather than an antagonistic one. However, note that instead of isolating one functional aspect, the theory attempts to see how cognition is related to effects and motivation within the context of an individual. For instance, there is a high likelihood that an individual will overreact emotionally and behaviorally to beliefs especially when that belief matters most to them.

The other thing that is important to note is that cognitive models also play a significant role in necessitating psychodynamic ideas. For instance, the construct of dichotomous thinking is said to be synonymous with the concept of splitting. Given the shift of splitting, this is seen as a disillusionment with caregivers whose nurturing qualities has been idealized.

Steps to cope with BPD

Did you know that learning how to cope with your loved one's BPD or yours can go a long way in helping you nurture a strong relationship while making progress towards recovery? Accumulating so much knowledge on the illness and then validating their feelings makes it very easy for you to help. It is important that you take time to learn about BPD, simplify the message, encourage responsibility, set boundaries, and take threats of self-harm and suicide very seriously to help you make a significant difference in how you relate with your loved ones.

It is important to note that as a loved one you are not going to fix BPD. However, you can help your loved one with BPD to find the treatment they need to make their condition better. It is also critical that you remember to find support for yourself if you have BPD. When you do this, you will forge a path towards healing as well as building a future that is beyond BPD.

The other thing you need to bear in mind is that BPD can be seemingly consuming. This is because it has the ability to weave itself into people's emotions, relationships and actions. If you are a loved of someone who has been diagnosed with BPD, there are instances when you will feel that the illness has become an insurmountable barrier that is standing between you and them. However, realize that it does not have to be a barrier. In fact, when you commit to learning how to deal with the disorder, you make it possible to fortify a relationship with your loved ones while offering the both of you the support you need to heal.

Here are some of the steps that will help you cope with BPD, whether for you or for the sake of your loved ones;

Step 1 Learn About the Illness

As we have already the fact and myths about BPD, it is evident that the disorder can have a very confusing diagnosis. In fact, there are so many misconceptions about what people suffering from this disorder experience. When you spend time educating yourself about this condition, the symptoms associated and its prognosis, you are helping yourself get a clearer understanding of what your loved ones are going through.

By reading and recommending this book to your loved ones and friends with BPD, you are helping change the conception of this disorder, one bit at a time. When you demystify what this disorder is all about, you are helping cut through the confusion, appreciate your loved one's struggles at a deeper level, and also feel equipped to offer support to those that need it as they go through their healing journey.

Step 2 Validate Their Feelings

One thing you will note about people with BPD is the fact that they experience reactions and intensity of their emotions that people without the disorder often find it very hard to relate to. In fact, you will realize that some people without the disorder don't even understand it and try as much as they can to talk them out of their feelings and emotions. Others go the extent of writing them off saying that it is irrational.

What you need to realize is that what they are feeling is real and is linked to the disorder they have. Instead of dismissing their emotional feelings causing them so much pain, try to put yourself in their shoes. Understand that by writing them off, you are just choosing to be counterproductive.

The truth is that you don't have to agree with them, but you can offer your validation. When you try to reflect back on what they have been telling you about their feelings and experiences, you will start to appreciate the kind of help they need and offer it as much as you can.

For example, you can tell them that you realize how much they are hurting and that they do not deserve to be in such pain and suffering. The least that you can do is show them empathy, compassion and respect while listening to them narrate and share their emotional feelings.

One thing you need to bear in mind is that validation goes a long way in helping someone with BPD feel that they belong somewhere. This is something that has become a central component of their treatment. When you ensure that your loved ones feel heard and loved no matter their condition, this will help them through recover as well as strengthening the relationship between you and them.

Step 3 Simplify Your Message

Did you know that a seemingly innocuous statement can be twisted into an attack? Unfortunately, this is something that happens often furthest from what you truly meant. Sometimes, it may feel as though you are unable to get through to your loved one because of the illness that comes in and stand between the two of you. the problem with this kind of distance is that it filters out your true intentions and makes your communication impossible.

To minimize the risk of this happening, it is important that when you are talking about the condition, and most especially sensitive issues, you must remember that emotions are likely to be too strong that the both of you are not able to do any high-thinking at that point in time. Therefore, ensure that you keep every sentence concise, simple and direct. In other words, what you are doing is using statements that leaves no room for misinterpretations.

While this may not guarantee that misinterpretations will not occur, it will facilitate clear communications to help you try as much as you can to avoid it from happening. Based on what the current state is, people with BPD may often distort what you are trying to say just to confirm to themselves their worst suspicions of you and your intentions.

Step 4 Encourage Responsibility

Do you have someone in your family that has BPD? If you do, then you agree with me that it is very easy to fall into a caretaking role. The truth is that it is natural to want to help the people that you care about for the sake of restoring normalcy to your relationship as much as you can.

However, the most important point to note is that encouraging responsibility is in some cases the most loving thing to do. Don't get me wrong – am not saying that you leave them alone to deal with their illness. The truth is that they need your support but it also means that you have to learn how to resist the urge to rescue them from the outcome of their own actions.

For instance, when they break something due to anger, it is critical that you try to resist yourself from jumping right in to fix them. If they get into debt, resist the urge to bail them out. When you do this, you are allowing them to experience the natural repercussions of their actions. This way, they understand better that they need help and they will be inclined to get the help they need. It also goes a long way in helping you to take a step back and not take responsibility for actions that are not your own fault in the first place. While this may seem counterintuitive to you at first, you will appreciate how empowering an experience it is for both of you.

Step 5 Set Boundaries

In the same way encouraging responsibility may feel wrong at first as we have mentioned earlier, so does setting boundaries. However, one thing that you need to bear in mind is that when you set and stick to boundaries, you get a much-needed sense of urgency and structure. It is through boundaries that you are able to encourage your loved one to remain accountable for their own actions and decisions. This in turn will keep you from having to endure unacceptable behaviors, so that you can ultimately strengthen your relationship with each other.

When you get down to setting boundaries, you must ensure that they are not only helpful, but also realistic. It is important that you try as much as you can to introduce new ideal in a loving and calm way instead of try to accuse and shame someone.

While this is something that seeks to ultimately help your loved one with BPD, be sure that when you start setting boundaries, they will interpret your actions as a sign of rejection. The thing is that thing will start getting worse at first, but eventually they will get better. Once you establish the boundaries, you must ensure that you stick to them however difficult it may be. Trust me, boundaries will be very beneficial to the both of you in the long run.

Step 6 Don't Ignore Threats of Suicide or Self-Harm

Threats of suicide and self-harm are some of the things that are very common among people with BPD. Several people consider these actions as a way of seeking attention and manipulating others especially your loved ones. However, what is important to note is that these threats among people with BPD are very real and should never be ignored whatsoever.

According to statistics, approximately 10% of people living with BPD die by suicide. What is even alarming is that at least 80% of those with BPD signal their intentions of suicide to their loved ones, especially by talking about it.

Therefore, if your loved one is threatening to take their own life or harm themselves in one way or the other, try as much as possible not to argue with them. Try not to accuse them of being manipulative or seeking attention. Instead, recognize the pain they are feeling and find a way to express your concerns for them in a calm way. As you do so, try to maintain the boundaries that you already set.

You could also call 911 for help or seek the help of a doctor. While it may not be your fault that a loved one with BPD took their lives by way of suicide or self-harm, it is critical that you try your best to keep them safe.

Step 7 Help Your Loved One Find Treatment

People who are suffering from BPD often are said to be reluctant to seek treatment for several reasons. Some of these reasons include the believe that what they are feeling is justified. The other one is that they have had negative experiences with their mental health care professionals in the past.

However, you must understand that the only way they are going to restore their emotional harmony is by ensuring that they have the support they need to make meaningful changers. This is something that they can get from a professional mental health treatment program.

For several people with BPD, several residential mental health programs give them the best environment to start the healing process. It is the immersive milieu and the intensity of therapy that allows your loved ones to be monitored continuously so that they rapidly progress to wellness.

It is important that you encourage your loved one to deeply explore their illness by using personalized curriculum of groups, individuals as well as holistic therapies among others. It is also critical that you encourage them to develop concrete strategies through such programs to enable them to make both emotional and behavioral changes. If they have a past history of trauma, connect them with programs that will offer them therapies that are focused on traumas to steer them towards healing.

Chapter 9 Find Support for Yourself

Let us all be real – dealing with BPD is not easy for you or even your loved ones. Several families with someone with BPD experience profound fear, isolation, and shame as they try to navigate through their illness. In such a situation, it is always important that your needs and emotional feelings do not get lost in your quest to help your loved one.

Take time to take care of yourself and nourish your body, mind and soul. When you pay attention of your own therapy and connecting with support groups of loved ones with someone with BPD, you will definitely get the guidance you need in dealing with this disorder.

Treatments for BPD You will be glad to know that treatments for borderline personality disorder come in a variety of ways it is just not popping pills. When it comes to treating BPD, there are various effective treatments in the form of therapy, medication, and even self-care. But the question you're probably wondering about is which treatment would work best for me or for my child? What should I know about the options that are available to me?

Doctors, therapists, and psychologists usually use a combination of treatments for someone with BPD depending on the severity of their symptoms as well as the period of intervention of treatment, early, mid, or late intervention.

Moreover, there could be some brief periods of hospitalization that are required for the individual to keep them safe. You'd be glad to also know that there are plenty of self-help tools and treatments that you can use on your own as a supplementary treatment for BPD. What can I expect from health-care professionals when I seek treatment? In , we mentioned that finding the right therapist, psychiatrist or doctor is a long process simply because you not only want to find someone who is an expert in BPD but also a doctor you are comfortable with you would be seeing them very often, so you want to work with someone who understands you and does not judge or ridicule you.

- A sense of welcoming

So the first thing to want or need in a healthcare professional is that they provide a welcoming stance for people with BPD

- You are entitled to get treatment

Just like any other mental or physical illness, if you think you have it or you are already diagnosed, it is your right to get treatment

- Respect and compassion

Health care providers should show respect and compassion when treating patients. They should be good at listening to your experience and problems, pay attention to your needs as well as take whatever feelings you are talking about- seriously.

- Professionalism and kindness

- If you have self-harmed, the staff should treat you for your injuries with professionalism. It is even better if they can arrange for you to speak to a trained psychiatrist or psychologist during this time. Questions to ask your health-care professional: Are you comfortable with treating someone with BPD?

- Can you refer me to someone who is experienced in treating BPD, if you are not?

- What is your main approach to treating BPD?

- Am I allowed to talk about difficult topics or sensitive issues with you?

- Am I allowed to express my emotions during our consultations?

- How do I get treatment for other methods you do not provide?

- Will you need to speak to my family/partner in my treatment process?

- Am I able to contact you during any moment of crisis?

- Who should I call if you are not available?

- Where else can I get reliable information for my condition?

- Are there any books or articles that I can refer to?

- What are your fees, and does my health insurance cover this?

Making decisions for your treatment Ultimately, you want to choose a treatment center or clinic that gives you all the information and assistance you need to help you deal with and overcome your disorder.

- As an adult, the decision is up to you to make about what treatments you want to engage in, depending on your financial capacity and availability. The doctor or provider responsible for your case should be able to give all the pros and cons of your treatment and mental health plan. Of course, if this is a medical emergency, the doctors themselves will make these decisions.

- If you are seeking treatment for your child, you can ask the doctor to recommend what is best for your child at the age that they are in and ask them about anything that you do not understand.

If you are an adolescent seeking treatment, again, the choice is up to you. However, the decision you make should be done together with a family member who is your primary caregiver. Would I be hospitalized immediately when I seek treatment? A person with BPD experiences intense emotional reactions, and these experiences often require immediate and intensive BPD treatments as well. Your healthcare provider, be it a doctor, therapist, psychiatrist, or psychologist, will require that you are admitted to a psychiatric hospital for immediate inpatient treatment if your symptoms need urgent medical attention. At times, you would be required to stay overnight, as well.

Partial hospitalization or day treatment is another option if hospitalization is required. These treatments are more intensive than the conventional outpatient psychotherapy, but they may not necessarily need an overnight stay. You could also be admitted into a day program if the doctor or psychiatrist feels that you are headed towards a crisis and need to be monitored or it could also be that you've been discharged from inpatient hospitalization but you still need some intensive treatment to ensure that your crisis does not return again. What Should be done in an Emergency Should you know someone, you love or if you are experiencing a mental health related emergency, it is crucial that you get help immediately. Calling 911, asking a neighbor for help, getting to your nearest ER or clinic is one of the few steps of getting emergency help.

If the doctor or psychologists find evidence that you are in danger to yourself or the people around you, they will get you admitted for a hospital stay at the inpatient psychiatric unit until the threat of the crisis has decreased and you are not harming yourself or other people.

A BPD safety plan is something you should put together for emergencies, which includes contact information of the therapist you are currently seeing, medication you are currently taking, next-of-kin to contact, coping skills and your triggers, so it helps you anticipate a crisis and have a plan on what to do and how to address your feelings before they turn into an emergency.

Treatment Goals While treatment differs between individuals, the bottom line is that they all have common goals in treating a person with BPD. These goals are:

- to help the individual overcome emotional problems from anger, depression, and anxiety

- to help the individual discover more purpose in life, from what their hobbies are, contributing to a cause, being part of a team

- to enable the individual to build better relationships

- To help the individual learn how to understand and live

to improve physical health. When should treatment start? Early intervention, even when an accurate diagnosis has not been reached. Early treatment is important so that the healthcare professional can kickstart a mental health plan to help the individual with BPD to manage some of their symptoms.

Diagnosis is, of course, important, but not getting a definite answer should not come in the way of getting treatment.

Many mental health centers and hospitals provide psychological treatments that are helpful in treating other mental health conditions, which would also prove useful and effective in treating BPD. If you already have a diagnosis, seek treatment immediately. In most cases, the doctor who has diagnosed you would already prepare a plan of treatment which you need to commit to. Therapy Psychotherapy

Also known as talk therapy, psychotherapy is a form of long-term outpatient treatment, and it is a vital aspect of BPD treatment.

- There are several types of psychotherapy that are used to treat BPD, and these are: Dialectical Behavior Therapy (DBT)

- As explained in the, DPT is the first level of psychotherapy that is found to be extremely helpful for individuals with BPD. Dialectical Behavioral Therapy is a segment of cognitive behavioral therapy which concentrates on beliefs and thoughts and how these can lead to our behaviors and actions. Through this therapy, individuals are taught how to handle conflict and distress as well as learn coping skills to deal with powerful emotions. Schema-Focused Therapy

- This is another type of cognitive behavioral therapy works on the basis that unfulfilled needs stemming from our childhood can lead to unhealthy forms of thinking about the world we live in. This therapy helps people to confront these misconceptions and behaviors and focus instead on positive and wholesome ways of thinking and coping. Mentalization Based Therapy

- To some degree, research has indicated that mentalization based therapy may help with social functioning, anxiety, and depression. Through this therapy, individuals would be able to identify various mental states, their feelings as well as their thoughts. Through acknowledgment, BPD individuals can also see how their thoughts contribute or influence their behaviors as well as the behaviors of people around them. Transference-Focused Psychotherapy

Some research and studies done on Transfer focused psychotherapy mentions that this type of therapy may be as good or even better than dialectical behavior therapy for BPD. This therapy employs the idea of transference, where emotions are transferred from one person to another. This transference is a key element that exists in psychodynamic therapies as well. Through transference-focused psychotherapy, the relationships between the BPD individual and the therapist are used so that the therapist will be able to see how the individual with BPD relates to the people around them. They can also use this awareness to enable the individual to respond efficiently with their family, friends and partners. Medication There are no specific medications solely to treat borderline personality disorder that is FDA approved. That said, research has given us information about some medications and how it can lower some symptoms related to BPD. In this case, medication can be extremely effective when it's used together with psychotherapy. Apart from mitigating these symptoms, using medications can also help with handling other coexisting conditions in mental health, which include depression and anxiety which are common in a person with Borderline Personality Disorder.

- Among the commonly prescribed medications that doctors usually give to a person with BPD are: Antidepressants: This medication helps with feelings of sadness but not so much for anger

- Antipsychotics: Usually the first line of medication given to a BPD individual and is helpful to address other problematic issues such as paranoid thinking, impulsivity and anger

- Anxiolytics: These medications are helpful because they help treat anxiety, which is a disorder that goes together with BPD.

Anticonvulsants: Also known as mood stabilizers, these help in controlling impulsive thoughts commonly associated with BPD

There could be a potential that the individual taking these medications may be addicted to it. Apart from medications, some research also suggested looking into our diets and have foods rich in Omega3 fatty acids.

Though that, no one study has found any significant or positive effects from making medication to help with BPD, except for the antipsychotics and mood stabilizers. The most useful and practical way to see which of these medication options are right for you is to consult your doctor or psychiatrist and tell them about your concerns or if you want to know which option is the best one for you. Your doctors should be able to iron out your concerns and come up with a mental health plan to get your symptoms under control. Self-Help When undergoing treatments for BPD, doctors and or psychiatrists will include some forms of self-help strategies that you can conduct on your own. Whatever self-help therapy you choose to do has to be from the advice from a qualified mental healthcare professional, but keep in mind that self-help alone is not the answer for treatments. You must treat it as complementary care in addition to therapy and even medication. A good mental health plan usually includes:

- learning and understanding your disorder

- identifying your triggers

- listing the symptoms, you have based on a specific period (sometimes symptoms can change)

- treatment plan and appointment dates for doctor's visits and therapy

- Medication dosage and frequency

- Emergency crisis plan of what to do, who to call

- Self-help strategies for whenever you need it

Healthy coping skills There are plenty of self-help resources that can be used for BPD in parallel with more conventional forms of treatments. From reading books, being part of online communities to help deal with your BPD, getting information from your healthcare clinics, and so on, these are just some of the ways to understand or make sense of the things going through your mind. Self-care for People with borderline personality disorder The major component of BPD treatment or any other treatment for that matter is that you must be committed and involved. Here are some things that you can do:

- Consult with your health care provider (and if necessary, your partner or family) to prepare for your BPD treatment.

- Make sure you are present for all the appointments and if necessary, with your primary caregiver if requested by your doctor

- Ask the healthcare worker about issues you're concerned about.

- Allow them to help you modify your everyday life and choices.

- Make sure you do the 'homework' which are tasks given by your psychologists as part of the treatment process

- Stay honest with your BPD. Talk about your problems and evaluate them so that you understand what makes you hurt yourself.

- Know how your emotions, desires, and relationships are handled. Learn how to deal with it rather than hurt yourself.

- Continue and never give up trying until you have control over your mental health and life.

- Obtain reliable and accurate information, especially when reading stuff off the internet. Whenever you read information related to BPD, just go through these details with your doctors.

Make a safety plan to get through bad times and inform your primary caregiver about it, so they know Coping with bad times There will be times when everything seems like it's crashing down on you, and you are unable to cope with too much. This not only leads to stress, but it could also lead to a BPD crisis. When you see your mental healthcare professional, they will focus on doing what is best here and now, which could include immediate hospitalization or overnight inpatient treatment.

At moments of crisis, there is no point in having in-depth discussions about relationship issues or past experiences. Your doctor's main agenda is to get you away from the crisis, which could also mean not talking about whatever that is bothering you at that time. These issues can be dealt with later. When you are experiencing strong emotions, try your best to stay involved with the doctors or whoever is at your aid during this time to find solutions to your problems. Remember that you must stay committed, and this often means there will be decisions you need make the people treating you will not make all decisions for you, and they will also ask you about your ideas and expectations in helping you recover from your crisis. Keeping yourself safe at times of crisis, you need to keep yourself safe even when waiting for emergency services to arrive. Earlier on in this, we detailed out things that a mental health plan should have, and one of them is an emergency crisis plan, which basically outlines what to do when you are in a crisis or in distress.

You can work with your therapist or psychiatrist to come up with a plan and essentially, it should include:

- Coping methods at times of crisis

- Who to call if you need to talk?

- Songs, movies, podcasts to listen to get your mind off things

- Lifeline support that you can reach out to

- The numbers of your psychiatrist/doctor

- Nearest hospital

Self-care box with scents that calm you, a journal, stress ball You can give a copy of this plan to your parents or friends in the event you cannot seem to retrieve it on your own. You can also use tools such as beyond blue and Project Air Strategy.

Apart from the ideas above, you can also include the information below in your safety plan:

- Your goals for treatment both long term and short term

- The problems you are working on overcoming

- Situations that can trigger feelings of insecurity, danger or distress

- Strategies that you've tried before that has helped get you out of distressing periods

- Strategies that have helped you from self-harming

Things that made these crisis moments even worse so whoever is helping you can avoid this Psychoeducation Another form of treatment for people with BPD is psychoeducation, where the main goal is to educate the individual with BPD, their families and partner to understand the illness. Psychoeducation also teaches people about the symptoms, why it happens, the options for treatment, and the recovery process. Psychoeducation is usually one of the main elements of psychological treatment. This treatment can be done in groups or individually and it includes written information, website resources, videos, meetings and discussions. The doctor in charge of your case will be able to give you access to psychoeducation programs in your area or region. Support that involves families Through understanding and knowledge awareness, families, friends, and partners will be able to know what kind of support to provide and in what way throughout the treatment process. If you have BPD or you know someone who has it, make sure to let them know that you want in on their treatment and that you'd do everything it takes to help them recover. If you are the one suffering from BPD, then make sure to nominate a friend, parent, or partner that you are comfortable with and someone who is reliable and trustworthy to be part of this journey with you. Treatment is easier when there is support and when everyone around you who cares for you has the same information about your condition and the treatment choices you have decided to be part of. Understanding is key to ensuring that everyone in your circle works towards the same goals of recovery. Psychoeducation is also good for the family that has the BPD individual because it can be overwhelming and distressing to see someone you love to go through violent episodes. It can also be overwhelming if you are the caregiver. I have kids. What happens to them if I have BPD? Nothing will happen so long as you go for treatment.

Having BPD does not make you a bad parent. One of the best things you can do if you have a child is to ensure that you keep working on your treatment, stay focused, determined, and not to give up. You also want to shield and keep them safe from any possible side effects of BPD. A parenting program can help you learn skills if you feel that you need help with parenting as a BPD individual. Again, your psychiatrist or other health professional would be able to provide this information. If you have a baby, there is no reason why your baby should not stay with you. This includes even when you need to go to the hospital. Coping Skills for Borderline Personality Disorder

Coping skills are important if you have borderline personality disorder. Coping skills can help you reduce emotion dysregulation, which refers to a poorly modulated emotional response that doesn't fall within the conventionally accepted range of emotive response. It can also help with other BPD symptoms.

What are Coping Skills?

Since Emotion dysregulation is an important feature of BPD, many BPD treatments emphasize the importance of building coping skills so you can better manage your emotions when they arise. What exactly are coping skills? They are simply healthier ways to address situations and emotions that result.

- It is important to learn new, healthier ways of coping. Using healthful coping skills can:

- Build confidence in your ability to be able to handle difficult situations.

- Improve your ability to be able to function well even when the circumstances are stressful.

- Reduce the intensity of the emotional distress you feel.

- Reduce the likelihood that you will do something harmful in an attempt to escape from the emotional distress. (self-harming)

- Reduce the likelihood that you will engage in behaviors that destroy relationships when you are upset.

- Reduce your overall experience of emotion dysregulation.

Different Types of Coping Skills?

There are thousands of different coping skills that you can use to manage stressful situations and the emotions that occur from these stressful situations. Here are a handful of types of coping skills that many find work.

Social Support

A social support network is made up of family, friends and peers. This is not the same as a support group which is structured a usually ran by a therapist. A social support network is something you develop when you aren't stressed. It can provide comfort when you know these people are there for you when you need them.

There are many benefits to having a social support network. It will help you have a sense of belonging and increase your self-worth. You can cultivate your social support network a number of ways. You can pick a cause that's important to you and volunteer. You'll meet others with like interests. You can join a gym, attend church, take some classes, or look online for a group that is about something you are interested in.

Building your social network is helpful with BPD because it helps to reduce your stress. Make sure you don't get involved in situations that drain your energy or a filled with drama. Avoid those involved in unhealthy behavior.

Relaxation Exercises

Relaxation exercises can help with BPD. There are a number of different ways you can approach this.

- Meditation – Just a few minutes a day can help to eliminate your anxiety. Sit straight with both feet on the floor, close your eyes and focus on repeating a positive mantra either silently or out loud (i.e. I am at peace). Let distracting thoughts float away.

- Breathe Deeply – Take 5 minutes to focus on your breathing. Sit up straight, close your eyes, place your hand on your belly, inhale slowly through the nose and feel your breath starting from the abdomen. Let it work its way to the top of your head. Exhale and reverse the process.

- Be Present – Take 5 minutes to just become aware of one behavior. Feel the wind on your face, feel the souls of your feet touching the ground, etc. Focusing on your senses reduces tension.

- Tune Into Your Body – You need to mentally scan your body and learn to sense the level of stress you are under. Lie on your back, start at your toes and work your way to the tip of your head. Note how your body is feeling. Do you have areas that are tight? Imagine each breath flowing to that body part. Do this for a minute or two.

- Laugh Out Loud – A good belly laugh is good for you and it will lighten your mental load. It reduces cortisol in your body, which is the stress hormone and boosts endorphins, which can help improve your mood.

- Decompress – Take a warm heat wrap around your neck and on your shoulders. Do this for 10 minutes.

Close your eyes, relax your neck, face and back muscles. Take the wrap off and take a tennis ball to massage away the tension. You do this by putting the ball between your back and the wall and then hold the pressure for about 15 seconds.

- Turn Up Your Tunes – Research has shown listening to music can reduce anxiety. Blow off some steam rocking to your favorite upbeat tunes or relax focusing on nature's sounds.

Behavioral Activation

Engage in an activity that takes your mind off the stressful situation even if it is just for a little while. This is very helpful for depression, BPD and other mood disorders. This can be a wide range of things such as going out for dinner, exercising, learning new skills, participating in new activities, completing household chores, working toward a specific work related goal, or working on improving your relationships.

Mindfulness Meditation

Practice mindfulness meditation, which helps you to observe and describe your experiences without judging or rejecting them. Mindfulness meditation is unique because it isn't focused on making us different from who we are now. Rather, it helps you to become aware of the moment. It teaches you to be unconditionally present. Mindfulness meditation works your body, breath and thoughts.

Sitting comfortably cross your legs in front of you. Cross them in a way that's comfortable for you and doesn't stress your legs. Rest your hands on your thighs, face down. Your eyes are partially open and your gaze rests on the floor in front of you about 4 feet. Don't stare; just let your gaze rest. Your front should be open and your back strong. Your mind will wonder, bring it back to your body and environment.

Now you'll work on your breathing. Rest your attention on your breathing. Feel it as it enters your body and exits your body. Let your breathing be natural. Sit for a couple of minutes doing your breathing. Finally, you'll work with your thoughts. As you sit you will have thoughts arising. When you notice you are so caught up in your thoughts that you forget you are sitting there, you have achieved your goal.

Grounding

Grounding is a set of strategies to detach from emotional pain such as anger or sadness. The distraction works by focusing outward rather than inward. You look outward to the external world. When emotional pain overwhelms you, you need to be able to detach so you can get control of your feelings and stay safe. Grounding will anchor you to the present and to reality.

You can do grounding anywhere, anytime. No one even has to know you are doing it. You can use grounding when you find yourself facing triggers. Grounding will put distance between you and your negative feelings. There are three main ways of grounding.

- Mental Grounding – Describe your environment in full detail and use all of your senses. For example, the room has white walls and 3 yellow chairs. There is a pedestal wood table and the room smells of pine.

- Play a categories game with yourself. For example, try to think of dog types, states that begin with C, etc.

- Describe an everyday activity in great depth. For example, describe the meal you cooked. First, I tenderized the meat, then I slice the vegetables, etc.

- Repeat a safety statement. For example, my name is Joe, I am safe right now. I am in the present, not the past."

- Use humor. Think of something funny to get rid of your bad mood.

- Physical Grounding – You can do a number of things.

- Grab onto your chair as hard as you can.

- Run cool water over your hands.

- Touch the various objects that are around you.

- Dig your heels into the floor.

- Clench and release your fists.

- Carry with you a grounding object such as a stone or a crystal.

- Focus on your breathing as you inhale and exhale.

- Soothing Grounding

  o Think of your favorites – your favorite animal, color, food, etc.

  o Say kind statements aloud such as 'you are a good person dealing with a hard time.'

  o Remember the words to an inspiring poem or song.

  o Picture people you care about.

Physical Activities

We've mentioned this already. Getting physical can be very helpful. It can be as simple as going for a walk. Whether you walk, run, dance or head to the gym, they can all distract you from your current emotional state.

Proper Sleep

It is important that you get a good night's sleep. Not enough sleep has a negative effect on your emotions. Getting enough sleep helps to calm you and it keeps you alert.

Read Something Happy

Reading is a great way to take your mind elsewhere. Choose something uplifting or happy to read. This is especially helpful if you love to read. For those of you that find reading a chore, you can still give it a try with something a light.

We've given you some great ideas to try to help you with your borderline personality disorder. They may not all work, but we're certain some will, so trial and error is your best course of action. When you find something that works, stick with it.

Chapter 10 The Different Types Of Narcissism

While we talk about narcissism in general terms, there is more than one type. In the real world, when you meet a narcissist face to face, there may be signs that matches the way a narcissist behaves because most of the time, they are a mix of the various types. As with typical mixes, there is always the dominant type mix with another.

To help you to determine which one is what, here's a brief rundown of each different type and their specific characteristics or personality traits:

Cerebral

A cerebral narcissist believes that they are better than anyone and that their intelligence far exceeds that of anyone else. They flaunt their intelligence and self-assumed superiority to be admired and envied by the rest. They know everything about, well, everything. They make it a point to have an opinion or suggestion for everything that you might throw at them. They will be happy to tell you stories that show off their sheer brilliance, whether the stories are real or just made up. They are happy to point out everyone else's failings and will look down on and sneer at anyone who is of a lower intelligence. Such people are so obsessed with their grey matter that they will go out of their way to take alarmingly good care of it, sometimes to an extent that it reflects badly on their health and physical prowess. Narcissism is very often associated with sexual stimulation. Cerebral narcissists rarely engage in sexual stimulation with others, as they prefer personal stimulation over the real deal. Therefore, it would not come as much of a surprise when I say that they prefer the anonymity and lack of intimacy that comes with pornography. For this reason, they may choose porn over close real relationships. Besides maintaining a relationship with such people is a Herculean task in itself. As they will always insist on being the intellectually superior one in the relationship and assumes the right to control the other person's thoughts, emotions and actions. Even then, these relationships will be extremely short lived as they are constantly looking for more superior people to associate with. Cerebral narcissists should not be confused with somatic narcissists.

Somatic

Somatic narcissists are more closely in touch with the Greek legend of Narcissus. They are all consumed by how beautiful they believe they are. You will often find somatic narcissists at a gym or somewhere else where they are working on their appearance. For them it is all about their body and physique. They can be constantly seen flexing their muscles and bragging about their success in sporting events. They expect their body to be the source of their narcissistic supply and so they dress up immaculately and keep themselves well groomed. Their narcissistic supply comes from how others react to how they look or from their sexual conquests – indeed, most somatic narcissists will have a long list of partners. They never cease to boast about their conquests in bed. Even though they may have bedded a lot of partners, most of the sex is bound to be cold and emotionless. Eventually, the word partner begins to lose meaning and they may be more aptly described as the victim. Cheating in a marital life is something that you shouldn't put past a somatic narcissist. He is happiest when his narcissistic supply comes from multiple sources. They are quite dangerous as they know how to manipulate people both emotionally and through sexual intercourse. This tends to scar their spouse for life if they decide to be in a long term relationship with them.

Overt

This form of narcissism manifests grandiosity. They are preoccupied about having outstanding success in a lot of areas, like brilliance, attractiveness, sense of power, ideal love etc. Since they have a large sense of grandiosity, they believe that they can only be fully appreciated by other people on their level of grandiosity. The overt narcissist always has to be in control of any situation. They are never wrong and they will never be shy about making it clear that everything is about them and that everything has to be done the way they want it done. Their egos are super-sized and they are not backwards in showing it to you either. The overt narcissist is able to cut you up, physically or verbally and will not show a single second of remorse or guilt.

Such people are interpersonally very exploitative and will not think twice before using someone to achieve their own needs. Although very arrogant on the inside, they are experts at masking their egotism within a false humility. They envy other people to a great extent and get terribly jealous of their achievements, possessions and relationships. They seriously lack empathy and this makes them unfit to work in a group. They are usually loners.

They may be seen as being overconfident and they are definitely extrovert in their behavior – in fact, it would easier to describe their personality as loud, obvious, larger than life, and somewhat oppressive.

Covert

The covert narcissist exhibits all the normal traits you would expect to find in a narcissist but with one difference – they want someone to take care of them. They are best described as the shy form of narcissism. He has grand fantasies similar to other types of narcissists but he lacks the drive to pull it off successfully. He is too timid to get what he wants and lacks self-confidence. He usually feels worthless at not being able to pull off exactly what he wanted. He faces large feelings of shame about the same thing. He rarely takes credit for his achievements. He openly admires successful people and secretly envies them. He is unlikely to accumulate appropriate friends and prefers to surround himself with more inferior type of people. Such people are hyper vigilant to rejection and humiliation. They could be described as parasites, living off other people. They will normally exhibit some signs of an illness that needs taking care of and that is why they can never be what you want. They don't want to take responsibility for anything and will look for a partner who is strong, successful, and intelligent, one that can run their lives while they don't need to contribute anything. Covert narcissists will sometimes pair up with the overt narcissist.

Unprincipled

The unprincipled narcissist does not have a conscience and cannot seem to tell the difference between what's right and what's wrong. They care very little about laws, values and conventions and stay just within the boundaries of the law. They exploit others without the slightest bit of remorse because they consider other people as inferior to them anyway. This unprincipled lifestyle makes them more than willing to risk harm and they are remarkable fearless in the face of danger. Their malicious and diabolic tendencies are easily visible and they get them into trouble with the department of law. They achieve gratification by dominating and humiliating others. These people never form an allegiance with anyone and so move from person to person with remarkable ease. They are alien to emotional attachments and do not feel the slightest remorse on ending a very promising relationship. The people they leave crumpled in their wake are very adversely affected, as the narcissist is usually very charming. These narcissists are exceptionally dangerous because for them, truth is only relative. They are masters of manipulation and deceit. They are very adept at scheming beneath a polite and civil veneer. Their plans are usually very cunning and worthy of admiration even though the means is hardly justified. They show no concern for other people's welfare, have no morals, scruples, and are highly deceptive when they deal with others. They will give off an air of arrogance and are driven by a need to get the better of everyone, just to prove that they are smarter. This kind of narcissist may be found in prisons or drug rehabilitation centers although there are an awful lot of unprincipled narcissists who never come up against the law. When in the vicinity of an unprincipled narcissist always be sure to keep your guard up. They smell insecurities a mile away and can easily turn you into a scapegoat for their next exploit.

Amorous

Amorous narcissists tend to be erotic or seductive in nature and they measure their entire self-worth around their, sometimes many, sexual conquests. Their relationships are often pathological and, as soon as they seduce someone, they are likely to throw them to one side while they look for their next conquest. They are never looking for an emotional connect but rather seek to inflate their already bloated ego by sexually dominating other people who they consider as trophies. The victim has more or less no idea that they are being used and sometimes they sincerely fall in love with the narcissists. However, the narcissist sincerely lacks any empathy and will simply throw them away like paper towels. This makes them outrageous heartbreakers. Not only are they often known as heartbreakers, they will also do some outrageous things, like pathological lying, conning their sexual partner out of money and other fraudulent acts. They use their sexual prowess to con unsuspecting people. The amorous narcissist is compensation for deep feelings of inadequacy. In most cases, they get away with it too because people hesitate to lodge a complaint against them.

Compensatory

Compensatory narcissists are constantly looking for a way to compensate for things that happened in the past, perhaps in their childhood and they do this by creating an illusion that they are superior. They tend to live in a fantasy world where they play the leading role in a theater that doesn't exist rather than living a real life. They imagine achievements in a bid to enhance their own self-esteem. They need an audience filled with people who will believe their deceptions and they are extremely sensitive to how other people perceive them, looking for signs that they are being criticized. They literally try to compensate for everything that they feel they were deprived off. Their agenda is similar to the other narcissists except that they are more focused rather than being guilty of random acts of narcissism.

Elite

The elite narcissist is, in many ways, very similar to the compensatory narcissist in that they are obsessed with their own self-image. The sense of self they create rarely resembles the real person but they manage to convince themselves and others that they have unique abilities and talents. They will, more often than not, turn a relationship into a contest or a competition where the only goal is to win, to prove to others that they are truly superior. This will happen with any type of relationship, be it family, work, or love. The elite narcissist is a social climber and will be happy to step on anyone who gets in his or her way. In a way, he is the most dangerous of all the types as he hides in plain sight so effectively that even the ones closest to him perceive him as a good and honest person. An elite narcissist is usually a highly successful businessman or business woman who has a very reputable profile. They consider material wealth and assets as a primary objective over true emotion. They are masters of deception and often use their talents to walk over other people. Being as cunning as they get, they usually have a legitimate and reputed business that they use as a front for all of their shady dealings. They are extremely protective of their personal space. If they get the slightest hint that you are a threat to everything that they have built up they will eliminate you without a second thought. They are ruthless and without remorse or empathy. They are concerned only with their wellbeing and the achievement of their goals. They will go to any length to achieve what they want.

Below are some of the narcissistic sub-types. These sub-types can be encountered from various people on a daily basis. Some can be annoying but tolerated, while some can cause emotional harm.

Conversational

Ever recall an instance where you are talking to a certain person, ranting or just randomly telling one of your everyday life stories to him? What's unforgettable is how the conversation always manages to end up with him as the subject and the victor? Annoying, right? Not only is it sickening to hear stories with always the same triumphant result, it is also annoying that they always make you forget what you are about to say due to their constant interruption.

This kind of conversation can happen between normal people as well, but it is almost always the case with people suffering from narcissism. There is even more aggressive conversational narcissist where they rudely cut you off while you were saying something, just so they can insist their own story whose lead character is always them.

If, by reading this part of the book, you are reminded of that one person who never fails to do this each and every time you are having a conversation, try to observe. Check out his other mannerisms, habits, or the way he behaves with other people Chances are, you have a narcissist who is sneakily turning all his friends into his supply sources.

Group Narcissism

Whenever the topic is narcissism, we are always presented with the idea that it is all about a person who cares for nothing else but himself. This is true, but it does not necessarily rule out the possibility of narcissism that can occur in a group.

In group narcissism, the narcissist individual is always a part of the group. Usually, the group is made up of narcissist people who mirror themselves and doesn't encounter any problem with having to co-exist with each other. They tend to become the narcissist supply source of each other and you will know that it is working out as the group acts as a narcissistic entity.

You see, narcissists have the tendency to gather or join each other in groups because it brings them comfort. This is due to the fact that they are all, pretty much, similar and share the same behaviors or habits. There's no questioning about why he behaves this way and she behaves that way, because they all know that they are trying to protect someone deep inside them.

Now, this group becomes a protector of the hidden real selves of each member. While this looks nice and beneficial for narcissist, this does not mean that they are already safe from the danger of self-destruction. It's always there, just below the surface.

Aggressive or Malignant Narcissism

This type of narcissism is your lesser type (like classic, cerebral, somatic, elite, and others) kicked up a notch because it becomes violent and psychopathic. Remember Adolf Hitler or Ted Bundy? They are categorized as aggressive types of narcissists.

Not all narcissists prefer to physically harm their supply source or victims. Most of the time, they just torture or abuse you mentally. However, when a narcissist becomes a bit too physical and performs murder, rape, or some other crimes with cold blood, that person can already be categorized as a malignant or aggressive narcissist.

Destructive Narcissism

So we have labels for, pretty much, every type of narcissist out there. Honestly, some psychiatrists do not exactly agree with these labels because identifying a narcissist is more than just knowing all the types and matching the several behaviors or signs dominant to that type.

What is more, there are also narcissists who are too clever that they are able to compensate for some of the behaviors in order to cover them up. That way, lesser track means lesser disruption to the facade that took them years and so much lies to build and complete.

There are also some people who cannot be also classified as a narcissist, but confuses you because they really match some of a narcissist's description. Now, why am I saying all these? This is because this type, the destructive narcissist, is one of those who do not technically fit the definition of a narcissist, but they also inflict plain on themselves and also shows general narcissist patterns.

Out of all the types, the destructive narcissist is the one that seems to be a bit irregular. It has some of the traits that can easily identify them within the various types of narcissist and all the while lacks some narcissistic traits that will solidify their being categorized as a narcissist.

Destructive narcissists usually have the most intense characteristics that a narcissist can have. These characteristics are set to ruin and destruct people around the narcissist and because of this, you can easily associate them with a pathological narcissist. However, the mentioned characteristics are fewer.

Sexual Narcissism

While this may raise your eyebrows as we have come to know that narcissists aren't exactly crazy about having sex with someone else, let us take a quick look at who these sexual narcissists are. Sex, when blended with grandiose becomes sexual narcissism. A sexual narcissist boasts pleasurable sexual skills, has sexual entitlement, and he also lacks sexual empathy.

The meaning? You get to have an intercourse with a sexual narcissist, but as always, it is for his pleasure and not yours. You may feel a satisfaction and this is no wonder because of the sexual skills of the narcissist. However, if the narcissist feels that he is already satisfied and you aren't yet, even if you are right in the middle of it and he wants to stop, he will stop.

He will only do it with you when he feels like it. So if a sexual narcissist doesn't feel like doing it, even if two weeks has passed already, you will never get one.

Another thing that you have to know about the sexual narcissist is that they have a big tendency to be an unfaithful partner. Big surprise! Since they feel like they have all the sexual skills, they also feel that they can do it with anyone as long as they are in the mood for it.

Acquired Situational Narcissism (ASN)

This narcissism sub-type is a lot different from the rest of the types, even the main ones, as ASN is acquired later on in life as an adult. All other narcissism types are acquired in the childhood phase of a person's life.

ASN can't just happen to anyone. One needs to have the narcissistic tendency as a child for ASN to be successfully triggered. This type of narcissism is triggered when an adult with narcissistic tendency suddenly comes across wealth, celebrity-status, or fame. Through this, the tendency suddenly blooms into a full-blown narcissistic personality disorder complete with signs, symptoms, behaviors and more harmful probabilities like the usual type of narcissism. The only difference is the age when the sufferer acquired it.

What feeds their narcissistic cravings are their fans, supporters, people around them, their fake friends, assistants, social media, and the traditional type of media.

Conclusion

After all is said, one thing you need to note about BPD is that it makes you feel like on you are on a rollercoaster. This is not just because you are impulsive or have unstable emotional feelings, but also due to a wavering sense of self – self-image, personal goals as well as likes and dislikes that are unclear.

The truth is that if you have been diagnosed with BPD, you are extremely sensitive. Think of it as someone who has an exposed nerve ending – such that even the smallest of all things can trigger an intense reaction. Once you are upset, it becomes very difficult to calm down.

While it is very easy to understand how such emotional volatility can contribute to relationship turmoil, the truth is that when you are in the throes of these impulsive behaviors, it is difficult to think straight. You find it hard to remain grounded. You will find yourself saying hurtful things that will trigger shame and guilt afterwards.

This kind of painful cycle can make it impossible for one to escape. But the truth is that it does not have to be like this. BPD is treatable and you can apply the techniques we have here to cope or deal with your condition or help your loved one through.

What you must understand is that breaking this dysfunctional cycle of thought, emotions and actions can cause distress. Well, no one said that it is going to be easy to change lifelong habits.

However, when you pause and reflect before acting, you will start to feel natural and comfortable.

The truth is that there are so many complex things that happen in the brain of someone with BPD. There is still ongoing research to try and untangle what it all means. However, the point is that if you have BPD, you will always remain high on alert. You start to feel scared and stressed over things that normally would not be considered scary of stressful by others.

You notice that your amygdala is always activated such that your flight-or-fight switch is on alert. Once it is switched on, the whole brain is hijacked and you begin to act irrationally. This trigger primitive instincts of survival that are not even deemed appropriate for such a situation.

While you may feel that everything is out of your control, the truth is that you can change your brain. When you practice new techniques of response, you create new neural pathways. Things like mindful meditation goes a long way in helping your brain to grow. The more you practice, the stronger these pathways become so that the next time, they are just activated automatically. So, instead of giving up, remain dedicated to self-recovery and you will eventually change the way you feel, act or think.

So, now you know what BPD is all about and what you can do to cope with the disorder – whether you or your loved one is diagnosed with the condition.

This book is your ultimate go-to resource for all your informational needs. Kindly leave us a review and comment down below on what your experience with this book was like. We value your opinion and believe that it will go a long way in helping us continue offering the best services to all our clients.

So, what are you still waiting for?

BPD is classified "the Good Prognosis Diagnosis" because, despite the fact that it is one of the more difficult mental health analyzes to contend with, numerous individuals have a high possibility of getting better or recovering altogether. If you have faith in your beloved one and stick by him during treatment, you may see genuine prizes. Many, numerous individuals who once experienced pervasive trouble in interpersonal relationships because of BPD are now healthy and completely functioning after treatment and a ton of self-work. Keeping a receptive outlook, working on your very own portion responses and reactions, and being honest with yourself about the substances of BPD may bring you to a fuller feeling of self and happiness in time.

Living with a borderline personality disorder is hard for the patient and friends and family. If you care about this person, support his or her treatment, figure out how to communicate viably, set limits, and make sure to think about yourself as well. Be patient and understand that BPD treatment sets aside some effort to work. Continue to give appropriate support, and your adored one will show signs of improvement.